Three Sisters

Three Sisters

A Comedy in Four Acts by Anton Pavlovich Chekhov

translated by Lanford Wilson

Great Translations for Actors Series

SK
A Smith and Kraus Book

ISBN 1-880399-28-8

Contents

Biography

LANFORD WILSON received the 1980 Pulitzer Prize for Drama and the New York Drama Critic's Circle award for *Talley's Folly*. He is a founding member of Circle Repertory Company and one of twenty-one resident playwrights for the company.

His work at Circle Rep includes: *The Family Continues* (1972), *The Hot L Baltimore* (1973), *The Mound Builders* (1975), *Serenading Louie* (1976), *5th Of July* (1978), *Talley's Folly* (1980), *A Tale Told* (1981), *Angels Fall* (1982), *Talley and Son* (1985), all directed by Marshall Mason, and the one-act plays *Brontosaurus* (1977) and *Thymus Vulgaris* (1982).

His other plays include: *Balm In Gilead* (1965), *The Gingham Dog* (1966), *The Rimers Of Eldritch* (1967), *Lemon Sky* (1969) and some twenty-five produced one-acts. He has also written the libretto for Lee Hoiby's opera of Tennessee Williams' *Summer And Smoke*, and two television plays, *Taxi*, and *The Migrants* based on a short story by Tennessee Williams.

Other awards include the New York Drama Critics' Circle Award, the Outer Critics' Circle Award and an Obie for *The Hot L Baltimore*, an Obie for *The Mound Builders*, a Drama-Logue Award for *5th Of July* and *Talley's Folly*, the Vernon Rice award for *The Rimers Of Eldritch*, and Tony Award nominations for *Talley's Folly*, *5th Of July*, and *Angels Fall*. He is the recipient of the Brandeis University Creative Arts Award in Theatre Arts and the Institute of Arts and Letters Award.

This translation of Chekhov's *Three Sisters*, was commissioned and produced by the Hartford Stage Company.

His play, *Burn This*, opened at the Mark Taper Forum in Los Angeles in January 1987 and opened on Broadway in October 1987.

His newest play, *Redwood Curtain*, opened in Seattle in January 1992 and in Philadelphia in March, and at the Old Globe in San Diego, California in January of 1993. It opened at the Brooks Atkinson Theatre on Broadway on March 30, 1993. A Poster of the Cosmos and The Moonshot Tape opened at Circle Repertory Theatre in May 1994.

He is a member of the Dramatists Guild Council and makes his home in Sag Harbor, New York.

Preface

Though Chekhov was not directly involved in rehearsals for the Moscow Art Theater's original production of the play, it was the first play he wrote specifically for that theater's artists. I wanted our THREE SISTERS to have a living playwright's involvement. After attending auditions and rehearsals, he would continue to "find" his translation within the process of the production. Lanford Wilson's fidelity to Chekhov is the most beautiful aspect of his beautiful translation. During rehearsals, his Russian text of the play was always open. The Russian-English dictionary became unglued with use. And his suggestions to the actors and me were insightful and helpful. The joy of discovering a THREE SISTERS with a playwright whose own plays carry so much of the same kinds of nuances, symbols, and character psychology was exciting. Lanford was ruthlessly conscientious about Chekhov's meaning. Certain parts of his translation seemed to be entirely new. As spoken by American actors, there were moments we discovered in the play that I'd never noticed before—signposts of truth and psychological depth.

Here are some of the things we re-discovered within Lanford's new translation: Chekhov's reputation as a realist is only partially deserved. He's as much a symbolist as he is a realist. Like the French Impressionist painters of his time, Chekhov builds up a large canvas by filling it with small, often inconsequential details. He provides pattern in lieu of plot. Action is woven into a pattern of recurring symbols and motifs. "Half enigmatic, half wonderful" is one character's description of life, and it could easily describe the play itself, for even as Chekhov arranges his details visually and metaphorically—even though he delineates his symbols with a keen, impressionistic subtlety—we are never sure exactly what is being symbolized. Therefore, the play's form actually represents the psychological dilemma of its own characters: "To live and not to know." THREE SIS-TERS is as stylized as a canvas by Monet or a score by Stravinsky, two artists who were the playwright's contemporaries. It "never quite asks to be accepted as a piece of naturalism," one critic has noted. Its reality is assured because of the playwright's selectivity of seemingly random detail.

These characters live life between two poles of experience: the Past and the Future. Their home is a kind of way-station, a limbo, a prison filled with windows aglow with possibility on one side and the aura of a dream-like past on the other. Their only reality is the Past, their only possibility the Future. Their Present is an enigma. Minutes slip irrevocably away as clocks tick and watches are checked. There is a marriage, two births, and a death during the course of the play, but these events barely ruffle the drama's detailed surface. No sooner does one of his characters express a nihilistic truth than another reveals a paradisiacal vision of hope; and the playwright treats both with a smiling detachment, so that we view the characters critically. Yet we identify with these officers, these genteel sisters, this schoolmaster, this young wife, etc. Like them, we continue to miss the moment.

—*Mark Lamos*

Introduction

The saga of this translation begins in 1980 when I was commissioned to write a play, which would become *Angels Fall*, for the New World Festival, to be held in Miami, Florida in the *summer* of '82. I said yes because it was almost two years away. I was working on two other pieces and, unfortunately, I didn't get the least hint of an idea for *Angels Fall* until April 1982—two months before the work was to premier in Miami in June, then play Lucille Lortel's White Barn Theater in August, and open the Circle Rep season in October. People have often commented on my prolificness (awkward word) and I usually have responded, "Thank you, I think," but I seem rather lazy to myself. I feel I work at about one third capacity. That year, first writing *Angels Fall* for Miami, then rewriting it all summer and most of the fall, I worked seven days a week, eight or more hours a day, with, for the first time, an assistant. I was working, finally, at full capacity—and I'm here to tell you it's no way to work.

By January '83, when the Circle Rep production of *Angels Fall* moved to the Longacre Theater on Broadway, (gorgeously produced, woefully underfinanced, with no advertising budget *at all!*), I was a burned-out puppy. I watched the already small audiences atrophy nightly during the months of January and February. Some masochistic fascination or loyalty drove me to attend almost every performance. When the play finally closed, I dragged myself out of the city, headachy and drugged with failure and fatigue, and my only wish was to lie on the beach and not have an original thought for a year. Be careful what you wish for. I didn't have an original thought for over two years.

However, I don't lie on the beach well. Into that summer came a call from Mark Lamos, artistic director of Hartford Stage Company. Would I be interested in writing a new translation of Chekhov's *Three Sisters*? The only thing I knew about translating was that it took a completely different part of the brain from writing original work. This proved true, practically my only assumption that did. The only thing I knew about *Three Sisters* was that it was my favorite play, and Chekhov had been celebrated as the first Russian to write plays in which characters spoke the way people actually speak. The only thing I knew about the existing translations was that I felt they were all unnecessarily stiff. The only thing I knew about the Russian language was that it used a different alphabet. I said I'd love to.

The plan was simple, and turned out to be simple in the sense of naive. I would get a copy of the Russian text, a tape of the Moscow Art Theater's radio-broadcast, commission a reliable literal translation, and buy a Russian-English dictionary. What could be easier? When my copy of the play in Russian arrived I knew immediately I was in deep yogurt. I could not tell "Act One" from "Olga." I had no idea where the text of the play began in the book. I fled to Berlitz, begging for help.

For over two months I sat across the table from a lovely lady three hours a day, six days a week. We spoke nothing but Russian. I came out of the sessions crazed and abstracted. I transliterated every word of every sign and headline in sight. Since it was 6 pm and I was at Rockefeller Center, there was not a cab in sight. I walked to Charley's (now Sam's), a bar in the middle of the theater district. After two drinks I could almost remember who I was and what language they were speaking around me. In the evenings I worked on written exercises. When people asked if I knew Russian, the only thing I could say was: I know all the words in *Three Sisters*.

I commissioned two translations, one by an American who teaches and speaks Russian, another by a native of the Soviet Union, fluent in English. What I really wanted, but I hadn't made myself clear, was a word-by-word translation, but it wouldn't have helped. I still looked up every word in the play. On the rare occasions when I realized I had read a sentence and actually understood it without looking up a single word, I danced a little jig in my workroom. It took me about a year to get through the play. It took Chekhov three months to write *Three Sisters*. He had the benefit of knowing the language.

I did everything I could do to understand the play, to understand every word, every sentence, and more importantly, the heart of the characters. But, not being Russian, not having lived among the people, not being completely familiar with turn-of-the-century Russian culture, there are things I couldn't hope to get exactly right. If I was writing in English: "I looked out over the amber waves of grain of this sweet Land of Liberty and all I could see was oil derricks," a Russian translator with an equivalent understanding of English might get the words right, and the meaning, and even the pretension and cynicism, but not the patriotic sadness of a popular myth gone sour. An equivalent patriotic Russian song, that meant something quite different, might convey the meaning much better. As much research as I might do, I can't pretend to know the equivalent Russian song.

Within that damning limitation, I tried to translate this play as accurately as I could. If the author says "fly" seven times in one speech, I translated it as "fly" seven times. If he echoes the word again half an hour later, so did I. As nearly as possible I have avoided phrases that were not coined in English before the play was written. (One I couldn't resist was "Shut up!") And I have tried to convey the sense of lyrical but natural, even casual, speech, that contemporary critics hated or loved in Chekhov's work. Sometimes I even added a line or two to make it clear what I perceived as the author's intention. In Masha's quotation of the Pushkin limerick ("A green oak grows in a sheltered cove, a golden chain wound around it..."), every Russian would know this poem was about as important and profound as "Hickory, Dickory, Dock". Still further he would know that the next line, in which the real symbolism lies, and also the key that this is a fairy tale, is: "And on that chain walks a learned cat." I couldn't resist taking the quote that one line further. For clarity, I hope, and also to cut Masha down to the foolish, self-centered, size I felt Chekhov intended.

Every once in a while I couldn't stand it, and didn't follow the author's lead. As with all the other translations, I presume, I first wrote Olga's: "I can't believe I'm free all night tonight and free all day tomorrow. Lord, that's going to be pleasant. And tomorrow night, free, and free the following day and free that night as well" (Or whatever it is.) All those heavy "frees" and days and nights piled on each other just got under my skin, and after two days of struggling with them, having lost all sense of what the silly woman was trying to say, I crossed everything out and wrote: "I'm off tomorrow; God that's wonderful. I'm off all weekend." I felt vindicated at the second preview, when two secretaries, at a Friday night show, sighed luxuriously in recognition.

The translation was performed brilliantly in Hartford. Andrei, beautifully played by James Eckhouse, really did play the violin. Tuzenbach really played the piano, and wonderful childish Fedotik really played the guitar. When they jammed together, for that one brief moment with everyone dancing and singing, "Oh you bower", the second act soared. In fact, I liked everything but my translation. Still too stiff; it still sounded like a translation. Dickens, who precedes Chekhov by a decade, doesn't sound like that; Synge, roughly Chekhov's contemporary, doesn't sound "translated". During the following year I worked to shake the academic (for want of a better word) sound from the damn thing. I still don't feel I've succeeded, but this is the best I can do within the confines of a literal translation, which was always my goal: *what would the play sound like if Chekhov had written it in English?*

Working so closely on the play for two years, I came to be astounded by the subtlety and suppleness of Chekhov's work; by the daring sexual heat and unabashed technical audacity. In the middle of a tawdry domestic scene at the top of Act Two, Ferapont, the hapless messenger, enters with a vaudeville act. If, in production, that scene isn't funny, you're doing it wrong. Irina doesn't have a good word to say about Solyony, yet she probably is infatuated with him. How can we sense this when there isn't a word to substantiate it? I had read that Chebutykin, who says he loved the sisters' mother, was actually their mothers' lover; perhaps he was even Irina's father. Ridiculous. Yet what else is the elaborate set up for the signal on the ceiling, but "May I come up?" Why else would the dead drunk doctor, confusing Irina with her mother, reliving the old days, knock on his ceiling, below Irina's bedroom, but to ask permission to join her? But then after two years you start seeing things. The play is forever deep, with startling juxtapositions of mood. No sooner does someone start to sing than they are asked to leave. If Andrei says life is disgusting, the old maid will enter in the next breath exclaiming, "What a wonderful life I have!"

Chekhov wrote his four major plays after hundreds of short stories, many of them essentially about these same people. He rewrote *Uncle Vanya* and *The Sea Gull* many times. He knew the people so well by the time he came to write *Three Sisters* he must have just sat back and listened to them sing.

When I was working on this translation I could converse (humblingly, haltingly) with the Russian cab drivers in New York. I was smugly pretentious ordering in a Russian restaurant. Only five years later, with no review of the language, going to a barber shop where everyone working there was Russian, I discovered I had lost it all. Alas, alack (what does "alack" mean? I've always intended to look it up), too damn bad, and serves me right. I'll have to start over from day one: I've just accepted a commission from The Philadelphia Drama Guild and The Seattle Repertory Theater to translate my second favorite play, *Uncle Vanya*.

—*Lanford Wilson*

This translation of THREE SISTERS was given its world premiere production by the Hartford Stage Company in Hartford, Connecticut in April, 1984. It was directed by Mark Lamos; the set was designed by John Conklin; the costumes were designed by Dunya Ramicova; the lighting was designed by Pat Collins, and the sound was by David Burdries. The cast was as follows:

OLGA	Annalee Jefferies
IRINA	Monique Fowler
MASHA	Mary Layne
BARON TUZENBACH	Chris Ceraso
CHEBUTYKIN	Alexander Scourby
SOLYONY	Michael O'Hare
FERAPONT	Frank Groseclose
ANFISA	Margot Stevenson
VERSHININ	Nicholas Kepros
ANDREI	James Eckhouse
KULYGIN	Robert Blumenfeld
NATASHA	Laura Hughes
FEDOTIK	Michael Kamtman
RODEZ	Mark Wayne Nelson
MAIDS	Donna Agee & Jennifer Chudy
SOLDIERS	Mark O'Donnell & S. Richard Simon

This translation was commissioned by Mark Lamos for the Hartford Stage Company and is dedicated to him and his wonderful cast.

Characters

PROZOROV, ANDREI SERGEICH

NATALYA IVANOVNA
His fiancee, later his wife

OLGA SERGEEVNA
His sister

MASHA SERGEEVNA
His sister

IRINA SERGEEVNA
His sister

KULYGIN, FYODOR ILICH
High school teacher; Masha's husband

VERSHININ, ALEKSANDR IGNATYCH
Lieutenant colonel, Battery commander

TUZENBACH, NIKOLAI LVOVICH
Baron, lieutenant

SOLYONY, VASILY VASILYCH
Captain

CHEBUTYKIN, IVAN ROMANYCH
Army doctor

FEDOTIK, ALEKSEI PETROVICH
Second lieutenant

RODEZ, VLADIMIR KARLYCH
Second lieutenant

FERAPONT
Courier for the City Council, an old man

ANFISA
The nanny, an old woman of eighty

Location: The action takes place in a provincial town.

Three Sisters

Act One

The Prozorov's house. A drawing room with columns, beyond which a dining room can be seen. Noon. Outside it is sunny and cheerful. A table in the dining room is being set for lunch. Olga, wearing the regulation dark blue dress of a high school teacher, keeps correcting her students' exercise books as she stands or walks about the room. Masha, in a black dress, sits with her hat in her lap and reads. Irina, in a white dress, stands absorbed in thought.

OLGA: Father died a year ago today, May fifth, your Saint's Day, Irina. It was so cold and snowing; I don't know where I found the strength to get through that day. You fainted and lay there absolutely moribund. But it's been a year, time passes, it's easier to look back now. You're wearing white again. You're just radiant. (*The clock strikes twelve.*) Just as the clock was striking. (*Pause.*) I remember the band playing when they carried father to the cemetery; they fired a salute to him at the graveyard. For a general, commander of an entire brigade, there weren't many people at his funeral. Of course the weather was no help; such a driving rain and snow.

IRINA: Why think about it? (*Baron Tuzenbach, Chebutykin and Solyony appear beyond the columns near the table in the dining room.*)

OLGA: I know. It's warm enough to have the windows wide open this year and there aren't even any leaves on the birches yet. But it was just about now, eleven years ago, when father got his brigade and packed us out of Moscow; early May, and the whole city was already in bloom from one end to the other; all Moscow was just bathed in sunshine. The way I remember it, it could have been yesterday and that was eleven years ago. Oh God! I almost shouted for joy when I saw all that light out this morning, I saw that it was maybe finally spring, and what I wanted more than anything was to be back home again.

CHEBUTYKIN: (*To Solyony and Tuzenbach.*) Fat chance.

TUZENBACH: I know, it's ridiculous. (*Masha, absorbed in her reading, quietly whistles a tune.*)

OLGA: Don't whistle, Masha. Really. (*Pause.*) Because all I get from being at that school every day and then having to tutor every night, is an unending headache. I'm beginning to think like someone who's already an old . . . Lord, I've literally felt it going, all my curiosity, all my energy, drop by drop, every day for the last four years. I think the only thing that's gained any strength in me at all is a dream . . .

IRINA: Go to Moscow. Sell the house, wind everything up here, and go to Moscow.

OLGA: Exactly, get back to Moscow as quick as we can. (*Tuzenbach and Chebutykin laugh.*)

IRINA: Andrei can study for his doctorate there just as well as here. He doesn't want to stay here any more than we do. The only thing stopping us is poor Masha.

OLGA: Masha'll spend the whole summer in Moscow, every year.

IRINA: Oh, God, let it happen! (*Looks out the window.*) What a gorgeous day! I don't know what's making me feel so light hearted. As soon as I remembered it was my Saint's Day this morning, I started thinking back to when I was little, when mama was living; I used to have so many wonderful ideas and get so excited. So many ideas.

OLGA: You're really just shining. I don't think you've ever been prettier. And Masha's pretty too. Andrei'd be all right but he's putting on so much weight and he doesn't carry it well. And I've just got older and skinnier every day. Probably from getting so furious with those girls at school. But not today, I'm off today, I'm home all day, I don't have a headache for a change; I feel absolutely rejuvenated. I'm only twenty-eight. Well, everything's good, everything's from God. But it'd still be a lot better to be married and spend the day at home. (*Pause.*) If I had a husband I'd love him.

TUZENBACH: (*To Solyony.*) You're just blathering and I'm getting bored listening to you. (*He enters the drawing room.*) I forgot to say our new Battery Commander, Vershinin, is coming over today.(*He sits at the piano.*)

OLGA: Is he? Good.

IRINA: Is he old?

TUZENBACH: Not really, no. No more than forty . . . forty-five. (*Plays softly.*) He seems all right; he talks an awful lot, but he's not an idiot at least.

IRINA: Is he interesting?

TUZENBACH: Yes, not bad. I should warn you he has a wife, a mother-in-law, and two little girls. His second marriage, by the way. He's making the rounds today, he hasn't seen anyone without telling them he has a wife and two little girls. He'll say it here. The wife is definitely not all there. She does her hair up in pigtails like a little girl; then she talks with amazing archness, philosophizing and attempting suicide with regularity. Obviously only to nettle Vershinin. I'd have left the woman years ago, but he's decided to tolerate her and complain about it.

SOLYONY: (*Comes into the drawing room with Chebutykin.*) With one hand I can only lift fifty pounds, but with both hands I can lift more than a hundred fifty. From which I conclude that two people don't have twice the strength of one, they have the strength of at least three and probably more.

CHEBUTYKIN: (*Reading a newspaper as he enters.*) If you're losing your hair, add ten grams of naphthalene to a half bottle of alcohol. Dissolve and apply daily. (*Writing in a notebook.*) Well, make a note. (*To*

Solyony.) Now, as I was saying: you close the bottle with a cork that has a glass tube running through it. Then you take a pinch of plain ordinary alum . . .

IRINA: Ivan Romanych, dear Ivan Romanych.

CHEBUTYKIN: What my little girl, what my darling?

IRINA: You're going to have to tell my why I feel so good today. I feel like I'm sailing. There's this enormous pale, pale sky and I'm gliding around in circles with these great white birds. Why should I feel like that? Why?

CHEBUTYKIN: (*Kissing her hands.*) My white bird . . .

IRINA: Because I woke up this morning, I got out of bed, I was washing my face, and all of a sudden everything in the world was totally lucid to me. I know how to live. My dear Ivan Romanych, I know everything. We were put here to work; man has to live by the sweat of his brow, I don't care who he is. That's the only thing that means anything. That's what gives our life a purpose. Without work happiness means nothing. Ecstasy means nothing! Oh, it would be so great to be someone who really does work, someone who gets up before dawn and breaks rocks on the roadcrew, or a rancher, or a teacher, working with children, or a railroad engineer . . . Oh, God! Otherwise why bother to be a human being at all. You'd be better off being an ox, it'd be better to be a plow-horse – at least they work – than to be one of those women who sleeps 'til noon, has her coffee in bed and then takes two hours to dress. Oh, that's hideous! The way you need water to quench your thirst when it's blazing hot out, that's how I need to work. And I just want you to stop being my friend if I don't start getting up and getting something done.

CHEBUTYKIN: (*Affectionately.*) I'll stop, I'll stop.

OLGA: Father drilled us to be up by seven. So now Irina wakes up at seven but she lies in bed thinking 'til at least nine – and with such a serious expression on her face. (*Laughs.*)

IRINA: You're so used to thinking of me as a child it seems incomprehensible to you that I might have a serious expression on my face. I'm twenty years old!

TUZENBACH: That incredible longing to do something. Oh, my God, do I understand that! I've never worked a day in my life. I was born in Petersburg, which must be the coldest most indolent city on earth and my family didn't even know the meaning of hardship, let alone work. I remember when I came home from the Academy, there was a lackey at the door to take my boots off. I was an incorrigible brat, of course, but Mother adored me. If anyone thought I wasn't so adorable it astonished her. They did all they could to protect me from work but they didn't quite succeed. Not quite. A cataclysmic change is coming. The clouds of a violent, life-giving, storm are gathering, you can feel it they're so close, and they're going to strip this laziness, this indifference, this contempt for work, all this putrid boredom out of our society forever. I'm going to go to work and in twenty-five, thirty years, every single person will be working. Everyone.

CHEBUTYKIN: I'm not going to work.

TUZENBACH: You don't count.

SOLYONY: In twenty five years you won't be with us, thank God. If you haven't died of a stroke in three or four years, I'll lose my patience with you and put a bullet through your forehead, my angel. (*Takes a bottle of perfume from his pocket and sprays his chest and hands.*)

CHEBUTYKIN: (*Laughing*) As a matter of fact, I've never done anything. I finished school and haven't lifted a finger since. I haven't even read a book; I never read anything except the paper. (*Takes a paper from his pocket.*) Here. I know from the paper that there was, say, someone named Dobrolyubov,* but what he wrote, no idea. God only knows. (*Sounds of banging on the floor.*) Listen . . . They want me downstairs.

---

*N.A. Dobrolyubov: (1836-61) important social and literary critic. His work contributed to the "superfluous person" theme in Russian Literature.

Someone's come to see me. I'll be there, I'm coming, I'm coming. Hold your horses. (*Goes out.*)

IRINA: Nobody's come to see him; he's making that up.

TUZENBACH: I know; from the look on his face, I think he has some fabulous present for you.

IRINA: Oh, no, that's awful.

OLGA: That's terrible; why's he so foolish?

MASHA: "A green oak grows in a sheltered cove . . . a golden chain wound around it . . . a golden chain wound around it . . . and on that chain walks a learned cat . . . " (*Stands up and hums quietly.*)

OLGA: You don't seem very cheerful today, Masha. Where are you going?

MASHA: (*Humming, puts on her hat.*) Home.

IRINA: Don't be like that . . .

TUZENBACH: Leaving the party?

MASHA: Oh, it's all the same, I'll come back this evening. Good bye, my love. (*Kisses Irina.*) Again, be healthy, be happy . . . When Dad was alive thirty or forty officers came to our Saint's Days, there was a riotous celebration . . . Today there's a man and a half and it's still as a desert. I'll go. I'm in a melancholy humor – unhappy me. Don't listen to me. (*Laughing through tears.*) We'll talk later; bye for now, darling. I'll go somewhere.

IRINA: (*Displeased.*) You're so . . .

OLGA: (*In tears.*) I know what you're thinking, Masha . . .

SOLYONY: If a man philosophizes, that might be philosophy, or it might

be sophistry, but if a woman – or worse, two – philosophizes, God
above, they don't fool anybody.

MASHA: What are you trying to say, you horrible, dreadful man?

SOLYONY: Nothing. "Before he even made a peep, the bear was on him in
a leap."

MASHA: (*Pause. To Olga, angrily.*) Stop that yowling. (*Enter Anfisa and
Ferapont with a cake.*)

ANFISA: Come on, old man. Come in, your boots are clean. (*To Irina.*)
From Protopopov, Mikhail Ilyich, at the City Council
. . . he's sent a cake.

IRINA: Thank you. Tell him thank you.

FERAPONT: Say what?

IRINA: (*Louder.*) Tell him thank you.

OLGA: Nanny, give him some cake. Go on, Ferapont, and have some
cake.

FERAPONT: Say what?

ANFISA: Come on, Ferapont Spiridonych. Come on, old fellow.

MASHA: I don't like Protopopov, Mikhail Potapych or Ivanych, or
whatever it is. He shouldn't have been invited.

IRINA: I didn't invite him.

MASHA: Well, that's something. (*Enter Chebutykin, followed by a soldier
carrying a silver samovar. There is a hum of astonishment and
dissatisfaction.*)

OLGA: A samovar. Oh that's horrible. (*Covering her face with her hands, moves toward the table in the dining room.*)

IRINA: Ivan Romanych, that's for an anniversary!

TUZENBACH: (*Laughs.*) What'd I tell you.

MASHA: Ivan Romanych, you should be ashamed of yourself.

CHEBUTYKIN: My darlings; my wonderful girls, you're everything I have. You're the dearest thing in this world. I'm almost sixty. I'm an old man. Just a lonely, useless old man. The only thing left of me that's any good at all is what I feel for you girls; if it weren't for you I'd have departed this world, thank you, long ago. (*To Irina.*) My dear child, I've known you since the day you were born. I carried you in my arms. I loved your mother.

IRINA: But why such extravagant presents?

CHEBUTYKIN: (*Through tears, angrily.*) Extravagant presents. Just shut up about it. (*To soldier.*) Put the samovar down in there. (*Teasing.*) Extravagant presents . . . (*The soldier carries the samovar into the dining room.*)

ANFISA: (*Walking through the drawing room.*) My dears, there's a Colonel here I never laid eyes on. He took off his coat and he's coming right on up. Irina, honey, you be nice and polite now. (*Going.*) God above and it's past lunchtime already.

TUZENBACH: No doubt this will be Vershinin. (*Enter Vershinin.*) Lieutenant-Colonel Vershinin.

VERSHININ: How do you do, I'm Vershinin. Oh I am so, so glad to finally see you. Lord, how you've grown. Ai, ai, ai, ai . . .

IRINA: Please, have a chair. We're very happy –

Act I

VERSHININ: (*Cheerfully.*) I'm so glad to see you. I'm so glad. Where's the other one? There were three sisters. I remember three little girls. I wouldn't remember what you looked like, but I'm absolutely certain that Colonel Prozorov had three little girls. I saw them with my own eyes. Where does the time go; ai, ai, ai, ai, where does the time go?

TUZENBACH: Alexander Ignatievich is from Moscow.

IRINA: From Moscow? You're from Moscow?

VERSHININ: Yes, I'm afraid I am. I was an officer in the same brigade as your father when he was Battery Commander there. (*To Masha.*) Now, your face seems familiar to me . . .

MASHA: But . . . yours, to me . . . no.

IRINA: Olya! Olya! (*Shouts into the dining room.*) Olya, hurry up and come here. (*Olga comes into the drawing room from the dining room.*) It turns out Colonel Vershinin is from Moscow.

VERSHININ: You would be Olga Sergeevna, the eldest . . . and you Maria, and you're Irina, the youngest . . .

OLGA: You're from Moscow?

VERSHININ: Yes. I had my training in Moscow, and started my service in Moscow. I've been stationed there for altogether too long. But now, finally, I've been given a battery here, and transferred here – well, as you see. I don't really remember you that well, I just remember there were three sisters. I couldn't forget your father, though. I can close my eyes and there he is. I used to come and see you in Moscow.

OLGA: I thought I remembered everyone, and here –

VERSHININ: My name is Aleksandr Ignatych.

IRINA: You're Aleksandr Ignatych and you come from Moscow. It's just

11

such a coincidence.

OLGA: See, we're moving back there.

IRINA: We plan to be back there by this fall . . . It's our hometown. We were born there. On old Basmanny Street . . . (*Both laugh with joy.*)

MASHA: It's just that the last person we expected to see was someone from home. (*Eagerly.*) Oh, wait! I remember you. You remember, Olya, they all used to talk about the "Lovesick Major?" You were only a lieutenant but you were in love with somebody – and for some reason I can't imagine they called you "Major." They used to tease you something awful.

VERSHININ: (*Laughs.*) Oh dear . . . "The Lovesick Major" . . . I'm afraid they did.

MASHA: Back then all you had was a moustache. Oh, you've got so old. (*Through tears.*) You've got so old.

VERSHININ: Yes, well, when I was the "Lovesick Major" I was very young; I was in love. Now, it's – otherwise.

OLGA: Oh, you don't have a single grey hair. You may be older, but you're not old.

VERSHININ: Well, nevertheless, I'm forty-two. When did you leave Moscow?

IRINA: Eleven years ago. Masha, don't cry, silly, or you'll start me.

MASHA: It's nothing. Where did you live?

VERSHININ: On Old Basmanny.

OLGA: But that's the same street we lived on.

VERSHININ: For a while I lived over on German Street because it was within walking distance of the Red Barracks. But on the way to the barracks you had to cross one of those gloomy old bridges, with the water under the bridge making these sounds . . . and when you're by yourself in a place like that, it's very easy to feel lonely. (*Pause.*) But there's such a marvelously wide river here. You have a beautiful river.

OLGA: Yes, and cold. And full of mosquitoes. It can get very cold . . .

VERSHININ: What? This is a good, strong Slavic climate. The forest, the river, the birches; all these wonderful chaste birches, they're my favorite tree. This is a delightful place to live. I will admit it's very odd that they built the railroad station twelve miles from anything and no one seems to know why.

SOLYONY: I know why. (*Everyone looks at him.*) Because if the station's close by it can't be far away; and if it's far away it can't be close by. (*There's an awkward silence.*)

TUZENBACH: Vasily Vasilych is our jokester.

OLGA: Now I'm remembering you. I remember.

VERSHININ: I knew your mother.

CHEBUTYKIN: She was a wonderful woman; her's is the Kingdom of Heaven.

IRINA: Mama was buried in Moscow.

OLGA: In the Novo-Devichy Cemetery.

MASHA: I can't believe it but I hardly remember what she looked like anymore. But I don't suppose anyone will remember us either. We'll be forgotten too.

VERSHININ: Yes, we'll be forgotten. That's just the way it is, nothing you can do about it. All the things we take seriously and think are so important and worthwhile, they'll decide aren't important in the least; probably forget all about them. (*Pause.*) What's more; we have no way of knowing what they'll think is utterly ridiculous. People were laughing at Copernicus or Columbus and saying their theories were worthless while they were hailing the flummery written by some ignoramus as absolute gospel. So it's easy to imagine our way of life, that we're so content with, will seem strange, primitive, ignorant, unsanitary, maybe even immoral . . .

TUZENBACH: Who knows, though? We might be living in one of the golden ages. People might have great respect for some of the things we've done. We don't have torture; there're no more firing squads, no invasions; all the while remembering, of course, that life is still so hard for so many people.

SOLYONY: Chicky, chicky, chicky . . . You don't have to feed the baron his kasha – just let him talk.

TUZENBACH: Vasily Vasilych, would you please leave me alone. (*Moves to another chair.*) You're becoming a bore. (*To the others.*) We see so much suffering around us everyday, and people would still have you believe our society has achieved a high spiritual and moral plane.

VERSHININ: Yes, yes, of course.

CHEBUTYKIN: Baron, I don't care how exalted you tell me our life is, people are still insignificant. (*He stands.*) Just look how insignificant *I* am. If you think I'm going to be consoled by learning that my life is lofty and understandable, forget it. (*A violin is played offstage.*)

MASHA: That's Andrei playing: our brother.

IRINA: He's the scholar in the family. He'll probably study for a Ph.D. Papa was military, but his son's decided on an academic life.

MASHA: It's what Papa wanted.

OLGA: We've been teasing him; we suspect he's just a tiny bit in love.

IRINA: With one of the girls from around here; she'll probably come over later.

MASHA: Lord, the way that girl dresses. It wouldn't be so bad if her clothes were just vulgar or out of fashion, but they're woefully pathetic. Some kind of bizarre, glaring, yellowish skirt, edged in a skimpy fringe, and with that she wears a crimson blouse. And her cheeks are just scrubbed. Scrubbed. Andrei is not in love, he still has some taste, I won't even entertain it. This is all just an elaborate joke he's playing on us. Besides, I heard yesterday that she's supposed to marry Protopopov, the chairman of the City Council. Which is perfect. (*Calling into the side door.*) Andrei, come here. Just for minute, darling. (*Andrei enters.*)

OLGA: This is my brother, Andrei Sergeevich.

VERSHININ: Vershinin.

ANDREI: Prozorov. (*Wipes sweat from his face.*) You're the new Battery Commander?

OLGA: Do you believe it – Aleksandr Ignatych is from Moscow.

ANDREI: Really? Well, I congratulate you; my sisters won't give you a moment's peace.

VERSHININ: I'm sure they're tired of me already.

IRINA: Look at the picture frame Andrei gave me. (*Shows him the frame.*) He made it himself.

VERSHININ: (*Looking at the frame and not knowing what to say.*) Yes . . . that's something . . .

IRINA: And he made the frame over the piano too. (*Andrei throws up his hands and moves away.*)

15

OLGA: He's our scholar and he plays the violin and he saws things out with his little fret-saw; he's a master of all trades. Andrei, don't go. That's the way he is – always leaving. Come here!

MASHA: Come on, come on.

ANDREI: Please leave me alone.

MASHA: You silly. Everyone used to call Aleksandr Ignatych the Lovesick Major and he didn't mind it a bit.

VERSHININ: Not a bit.

MASHA: But I want to call you the Lovesick Fiddler.

IRINA: Or the Lovesick Professor.

OLGA: He's in love; Andriushka's in love! Andriushka's in love!

IRINA: (*Clapping her hands.*) Bravo. Bravo, again. Andriushka's in love!

CHEBUTYKIN: (*Coming behind Andrei and putting both arms around his waist.*): "For love alone has nature put us here!" (*Laughs, still holds the newspaper.*)

ANDREI: All right, enough, enough. I didn't get to sleep all night last night and I'm not what you might call myself. I read 'til four in the morning, then I went to bed, but nothing happened. I kept thinking about one thing or another, and it gets light so early here; the sun just invades my room. There's a book, I'd like to translate from English this summer before we go to Moscow.

VERSHININ: You know English, then?

ANDREI: Yes, Father, may he rest in peace, burdened us with an education. I know it's ridiculous, but in the year since he died I've done nothing but eat. As if my body had finally been freed from bondage. Thanks to Father my sisters and I know French, German, English, Irina even knows Italian. But Lord, what it cost us.

MASHA: Knowing three languages in this town's an unnecessary luxury. Not even a luxury, just an extra appendage, like having six fingers. What we know is a lot of uselessness.

VERSHININ: Oh my goodness. (*Laughs.*) What you know is a lot of uselessness. I can't imagine a town anywhere . . . I don't think there could even be a town . . . that was so cheerless and so dreary that it didn't need educated and intelligent people. All right, say that in all this town, of a hundred thousand population, which admittedly is backward and coarse, they're only three like you. You certainly can't hope to conquer this entire ignorant mass that surrounds you. In the course of your lives you'll be forced to give way here, little by little there, 'til eventually you'll be overwhelmed by this ocean of one-hundred-thousand-strong. You'll be lost at sea, no question, absolutely vanish, but not quite without a trace: because, don't think someone like you won't have an influence. After you've gone they'll be others who come. Perhaps only six, at first; then twelve, then more, and more, until one day most of the people in town will be people such as the three of you. In two hundred years, three hundred years, life on earth will be unimaginably beautiful, we'd be astonished. Man yearns for a better life and if he doesn't have it now, then he has to envision it, be open for it, dream about it, prepare for it. So it's incumbent upon him to see more and know more than his father and his grandfather saw and knew. (*Laughs.*) And you complain that what you know is a lot of uselessness.

MASHA: (*Taking off her hat.*) I'll stay for lunch. (*Andrei, unnoticed, has left the room.*)

IRINA: Someone should have written that down.

TUZENBACH: I'm sure you're right. Life will be beautiful, even astonishing, one day. And we can be a part of it even from this distance, as you say, we can help lay the way. And what we have to do to prepare for that future is go to work.

VERSHININ: (*Gets up.*) Yes. Look at all the flowers! (*Looking around.*) And your beautiful home. I'm so envious! I've spent my entire life banging around in apartments with two chairs, one divan and a stove that generates only smoke. My life has been less for not having flowers like these. (*Rubs his hands.*) Ah, well . . . nothing to be done about that.

TUZENBACH: Yes. We've got to go to work. I know you think, well, typically, the sentimental German is off again, but I'm – word of honor – Russian. I don't even know German. My father was Russian Orthodox . . . (*Pause.*)

VERSHININ: (*Pacing.*) I often wonder what it would be like if we could begin our lives over again – knowing that we were being given the opportunity of a fresh start. What if the life we've lived so far was only a rough draft, and our new life would be the fair copy. I know we'd certainly try to keep from just repeating the same old choices. At least we'd want to create a new *mise-en-scene*, I'd have a home like this, with these flowers, and with all this light. I have a wife now and two little girls, and then the little lady is ill-disposed, and so on and so on, well – but if I could begin my life over again I wouldn't get married . . . no, no!

KULYGIN: (*Enters in a teacher's uniform.*) Dear sister, congratulations on your Saint's Day. I want to wish you sincerely, with all my heart, health and everything one could want for a girl your age. I've brought a book for you. (*Gives her a book.*) It's the history of our school over the past fifty years, written by me. A trifling book, of course, written in spare moments, but you might enjoy it. Greetings everyone. (*To Vershinin.*) I'm Kulygin, one of the teachers at the school here, and on the City Council. (*To Irina.*) There's a complete list there of everyone who's graduated from our school in the last fifty years. *Feci, quod, poturi, faciant meliora potentes.*[I've done what I can, if others can do better, let them.] (*Kisses Masha.*)

IRINA: But you gave me this book last Easter.

KULYGIN: (*Laughing.*) Impossible. In that case, give it back, or better still
. . . give it to the Colonel here. Take it, Colonel; read it when you're
bored sometime.

VERSHININ: Thank you very much. (*Preparing to leave.*) Well, it's been
wonderful meeting you.

OLGA: You're leaving? don't go.

IRINA: Stay for lunch, please.

OLGA: Yes, please.

VERSHININ: (*Bows.*) I seem to have barged into a Saint's Day party.
Forgive me, I didn't realize. I didn't even congratulate you . . .
(*Walks off with Olga into the dining room.*)

KULYGIN: My friends, it's Sunday, the day of rest, so let's rest and enjoy
ourselves, each as best he can and as best he deserves. It's time to roll
up the carpets for summer, store them 'til winter. Put them in moth
balls . . . The Romans were healthy because they knew when to work
and they knew when to play. They had a *mens sana in corpore sane.*
[Healthy spirit in a healthy body] Their lives followed a definite daily
routine, a form. Our principal always says: the important thing in
every life is form . . . a thing wanders from its routine, loses its form,
and it's finished. And it's the same for us, every day. (*Puts his arm
around Masha's waist, laughing.*) Masha loves me. My wife loves me.
The draperies have to go out with the carpets. I'm cheerful today, I
feel wonderful. Masha, we have to be at the principal's at four
o'clock. There's an outing for the teachers and their families.

MASHA: I'm not going.

KULYGIN: (*Distressed.*) Masha, Darling, why not?

MASHA: I'll tell you later. (*Angry.*) Oh, fine, I'll go, just leave me alone, please. (*Moves away.*)

KULYGIN: Then we'll spend the evening at the principal's. Even though he's not really well, he makes a wonderful effort to be sociable. He's a fine, enlightened person, marvelous man. After the staff meeting yesterday he said to me, "I'm tired, Fyodor Ilych, I'm tired." (*Looks at the clock, then his watch.*) Your clock is seven minutes fast. Yes, he said, "I'm tired." (*Sounds of a violin are heard offstage.*)

OLGA: Ladies and gentlemen, lunch is served. It's pirog.

KULYGIN: Olga, my dear, dear sweet Olga. I worked all day yesterday from the crack of dawn 'til eleven o'clock. I was utterly exhausted, but today I feel like a fortunate man. (*Goes to the table in dining room.*) My dear . . .

CHEBUTYKIN: (*Puts newspaper in his pocket, combs his beard.*) Pirog, splendid.

MASHA: Only look here, you. Don 't start drinking today. You hear me? It's not good for you.

CHEBUTYKIN: Nonsense, I haven't done any serious drinking in two years. (*Impatiently.*) Anyway, my dear, what possible difference could it make.

MASHA: All the same don't you dare drink. Don't you dare. (*Angrily, but making sure her husband doesn't hear.*) Damn it to hell, another excruciating evening at the principal's.

TUZENBACH: If I were you I wouldn't go; simple as that.

CHEBUTYKIN: Don't go, darling.

MASHA: Sure, don't go . . . this damnable, intolerable life . . . (*Walks into dining room.*)

CHEBUTYKIN: (*Going after her.*) No, no . . .

SOLYONY: (*Going into dining room.*) Chicky, chicky, chicky . . .

TUZENBACH: Enough, Solyony. Stop it.

SOLYONY: Chicky, chicky, chicky . . .

KULYGIN: (*Cheerfully.*) To your health, Colonel! I'm a teacher and as Masha's husband, one of the family here . . . she's sweet, very sweet.

VERSHININ: I'll have the dark vodka . . . (*Drinks.*) Your health. (*To Olga.*) You have a very pleasant home. (*Only Irina and Tuzenbach are left in the drawing room.*)

IRINA: Masha's in a terrible mood today. She was only eighteen when she got married and he seemed like the cleverest man in the world. Not any more. He's very kind but he's not very clever.

OLGA: (*Impatiently.*) Andrei, come on.

ANDREI: (*Off.*) Coming. (*He enters and goes directly to the table.*)

TUZENBACH: What are you thinking?

IRINA: Nothing. I don't like your Solyony; he scares me to death. He says such stupid things.

TUZENBACH: I know, he's a very strange man. I feel sorry for him. He drives me crazy, of course, but most of the time I feel sorry for him. I think he's just terribly shy, odd as that sounds. When there's only the two of us he's sensitive, he's clever as anyone; unfortunately in a crowd he's a bully and a lout. Don't go. Wait 'til they've settled down at the table. Let me be alone with you a minute. What are you thinking? (*Pause.*) You're twenty, I'm not even thirty yet. We have so many years ahead of us; a long, long line of days filled with my love for you . . .

IRINA: Nikolai Lvovich, don't talk to me about love.

TUZENBACH: (*Not listening.*) I have a passionate thirst for life, to struggle, to work; and this thirst that I have is so mixed up with the way I love you, Irina, that because you're so beautiful, it makes me think that life is beautiful too. What are you thinking?

IRINA: You may say life is beautiful. Fine, but I don't see any evidence of it. Life hasn't been beautiful for us three sisters. Life has stifled us like weeds. I'm crying; what a useless thing to do. (*Quickly wipes her eyes, smiles.*) The only thing that's useful is work. That's why we're so depressed, why we have such a dismal view of life; we have no idea what it is to really work. Our parents thought they were too good to work. (*Enter Natalya Ivanovna, wearing a pink dress with a green sash.*)

NATASHA: They've already gone to the table, I'm late. (*Glances in mirror and straightens herself.*) The hair's not too bad . . . (*Seeing Irina.*) Dear Irina Sergeevna, congratulations! (*Kisses her vigorously.*) You have so much company . . . I get self-conscious. Hello, Baron!

OLGA: (*Enters the drawing room.*) Ah, here's Natasha. Hello, dear. (*They kiss.*)

NATASHA: Congratulations. There are so many people here, I get embarrassed.

OLGA: Don't be silly, everyone's family. (*Dropping her voice, alarmed.*) You're wearing a green belt with that dress? Darling, not right at all.

NATASHA: Is is supposed to be an omen?

OLGA: No, it just doesn't match anything . . . it's just peculiar . . .

NATASHA: (*Crying.*) It's peculiar? But it's not really green. It's just sort of drab. (*She follows Olga to the dining room. In the dining room they sit down to lunch. The drawing room is empty.*)

KULYGIN: Irina, I wish for you, a nice eligible young man. It's about time you got married.

CHEBUTYKIN: And a young man for you, Natalya Ivanovna.

KULYGIN: I have a feeling Natalya Ivanovna has already found herself a young man.

MASHA: I might have one glass of wine. Oh, life is the berries! Too bad the season's so short, but what the hell!

KULYGIN: For that you get a C-minus in deportment.

VERSHININ: This is an excellent aperitif. What's it distilled from?

SOLYONY: Cockroaches.

IRINA: Oh, no, oh, that's disgusting. (*Ready to cry.*)

OLGA: Ladies and gentlemen, there's going to be turkey and apple tart for supper. Thank the Lord I'm home all day and home all night, and if you'll just join us for supper this evening everything will be perfect.

VERSHININ: If that includes me I'd like to very much.

OLGA: Please, please.

NATASHA: They're not formal.

CHEBUTYKIN: "For love alone has nature put us here." (*Laughs.*)

ANDREI: (*Angry.*) Stop it, gentlemen. I think you'd be getting pretty sick of that. (*Fedotik and Rodez enter with a large basket of flowers.*)

FEDOTIK: They're already in the middle of lunch.

RODEZ: (*Loudly, rather affected.*) Having lunch? Good Lord, they've already started to eat.

FEDOTIK: Wait a minute! (*Takes a photograph.*) One! Just a second more. (*Takes another photograph.*) Two. Now I'm set. (*They carry the basket into the living room where they're greeted noisily.*)

RODEZ: (*Loudly.*) Congratulations. I wish you everything, absolutely everything. What a glorious day. Hasn't it been wonderful? I was out running with some of the boys all morning. I'm the coach at the school here.

FEDOTIK: It's all right to move, Irina Sergeevna; it doesn't matter. (*Takes another.*) You look absolutely fascinating today. Thank you. (*Takes a top from his pocket.*) I've brought you a top. It has a wonderful sound . . .

IRINA: It's pretty.

MASHA: "An oak tree grows in a sheltered cove . . . a golden chain wound around it . . . a golden chain wound around it . . . and on that chain walks a learned cat . . . " (*Tearful.*) Why on earth do I keep saying that? Those words have been nagging me all day.

KULYGIN: Thirteen at table!

RODEZ: (*Loudly.*) Gentlemen! I certainly hope you attach no significance to those old wives' tales. (*Laughter.*)

KULYGIN: When there are thirteen people at the table, it means that one of the company is in love. By any chance could that be you, Ivan Romanych . . . (*Laughter.*)

CHEBUTYKIN: I'm just an old sinner. But I can't imagine why Natalya Ivanovna is getting so flustered. (*Loud laughter, Natasha runs out of the dining room into the drawing room, with Andrei following her.*)

ANDREI: Please. Don't pay attention to them, don't. Wait . . . please.

Act I

NATASHA: I'm so embarrassed. They keep making fun of me and I don't know what I'm doing wrong. I don't want to be impolite and leave the table, but I can't help it. I can't.

ANDREI: Darling, please, I beg you, don't be upset. Really, truly, they're only joking. They don't mean it. My dear, my darling, really they're all kind, good hearted people, they love us both. Come over by the window where they can't see us . . . (*Looks around.*)

NATASHA: I'm not used to being around so many people . . .

ANDREI: You're so young, you're so wonderfully, astonishingly young. Don't be upset, darling, you're so dear. Believe me, believe . . . I feel so good, my soul is just so full of love and joy . . . Oh, they can't see us! They can't see. Why, why did I fall in love with you; when did I fall in love? I don't understand anything. My dear, my darling, my innocent child – Will you marry me? I love you, love . . . like no one, never . . . (*Kisses her. Two officers enter the room and, seeing Natasha and Andrei kissing, stop in astonishment.*)

CURTAIN

Act Two

The same. Eight p.m. From the street is heard the faint sound of someone playing an accordion. The stage is dark. Natasha enters in her dressing gown carrying a candle. She walks across the stage and stops at the door to Andrei's room.

NATASHA: Andryusha? What are you doing? You reading? Never mind, I was only . . . (*Walks on, opens another door, looks in, closes door.*) No light . . .

ANDREI: (*Enters with a book in his hand.*) What, Natasha?

NATASHA: I was just making sure there's no light. The staff aren't themselves during carnival time; you have to double-check everything they do. I came through the dining room at midnight last night, someone had left a candle. None of them would admit to it, of course. What time do you have?

ANDREI: (*Looks at his watch.*) Eight-fifteen.

NATASHA: Irina must still be at the telegraph office; they work too hard. Olga has a faculty meeting I guess, or something; neither one of them's home. (*Sigh.*) I tried to tell her this morning, "Irina, darling, you've got to start taking care of yourself," but she won't listen. Eight-fifteen? I don't understand what's making Bobik so cold; I hope he's not coming down with something. Yesterday he was burning up, today he's been cold all over. It really scares me.

ANDREI: The boy's fine, Natasha, it's nothing.

NATASHA: And I'm not happy with the way he's been eating. I really get scared. And now they tell me the Revelers are supposed to be here at nine o'clock; I think it'd be better if they just skipped us this year, Andryusha.

ANDREI: I wouldn't know . . . I think they've already been asked.

NATASHA: The little silly woke up this morning and he looked up at me and all of a sudden he got this big smile on his face, and I said, "You recognized me, didn't you, Bobik? How do you do? How do you do, baby?" And he just laughed. They really do, babies understand everything. That's all right, then, Andryusha, I'll let them know we really can't have the Revelers; not this evening.

ANDREI: (*Indecisively.*) Fine, only that's something my sisters will have to decide; that's their domain.

NATASHA: Their's too, I know, I'll tell them. They're always so considerate. (*She moves away.*) I've got you some yogurt for supper. The doctor said that's all you can have if you're ever going to lose weight. (*Stops.*) Bobik's cold. I'm afraid it's the room he's in. I just think 'til the weather warms up we're going to have to find another room for him. The room that should be the nursery, of course, is Irina's room; it's the only room that's dry . . . it gets the sun all day . . . we could tell her to move in with Olga for a while; she's never here during the day, anyway, she's only home at night. (*Pause.*) Andryusha, why are you so quiet?

ANDREI: Just preoccupied . . . anyway, I don't have anything to say.

NATASHA: I know . . . Now, what did I want to tell you? Oh. Ferapont wants to see you; he has something from the council.

ANDREI: (*Yawning.*) Tell him to come in. (*Natasha leaves. Andrei, bending over the candle that she forgot, reads a book. Ferapont enters, wearing an old shabby overcoat with the collar turned up, a scarf covering his ears.*) Hello, my friend, what's on your mind?

FERAPONT: There's a book from Chairman Protopopov and some papers about something. (*Gives Andrei the book and the packet.*)

ANDREI: All right, thank you. How come you're working so late? It's nearly nine o'clock.

FERAPONT: Say what?

ANDREI: (*Louder.*) You're working late. It's nearly nine o'clock.

FERAPONT: Yes, sir. It was still light when I got here; nobody'd let me in. They said the Master's busy; well, that's that. Busy's busy. I got no plans. (*Thinking Andrei has spoken.*) Say what?

ANDREI: Nothing (*Looks at the book.*) Tomorrow's Friday? I'll go in anyway; there's no meeting but it's so boring at home, I might as well get something done. (*Pause.*) You know what, grandpa? Life is a slippery, fickle business. I was so bored today I started looking through some of my old lecture notes from school. Now, that's funny. My God, I'm a secretary for the City Council. Protopopov is Chairman of the Council and I'm an employee. But, then, one day I can hope to be elevated to the position of Member of the Council myself. That's all there is to look forward to for someone who dreams every night that I'm a renowned scholar, professor at the University of Moscow, pride and joy of all Russia!

FERAPONT: I can't say. Hearing's no good.

ANDREI: Yes, well, maybe if you could hear I wouldn't be talking to you. My wife certainly doesn't understand anything I say – I have to talk to someone; my sisters just panic me, I don't know, they just laugh; they seem to enjoy humiliating me. I don't like bars that much, I don't even drink, but I'd give anything, and love it, to be sitting right now in the dining room of Testov's in Moscow. Or in the Grand Moscow Hotel.

FERAPONT: 'While back there was this contractor over at the City Council; said a bunch of businessmen got together in Moscow and ate bliny. Way he told it one of the men ate forty of them and died. Forty or fifty. Don't remember which.

ANDREI: You can go to an enormous restaurant in Moscow, you may not know anyone, no one knows you, you still have the feeling you belong. Here you know everyone, everyone knows you and you're an alien . . . an alien . . . alien and alone.

FERAPONT: Say what? (*Pause.*) This same contractor told how – he might've been lying – but he said they'd stretched a wire from one end of Moscow to the other.

ANDREI: For what?

FERAPONT: I can't figure it out. The contractor said it, I didn't.

ANDREI: That's ridiculous. (*Reads book.*) Have you ever been to Moscow?

FERAPONT: (*After a pause.*) Never have. It wasn't God's will. (*Pause.*) Can I go now?

ANDREI: Of course you may. Be well. (*Ferapont leaves.*) You can pick these up tomorrow; no reason to stay now. (*Pause.*) He's gone. (*A bell rings.*) Well, what do you expect? (*He stretches and slowly walks toward his room. Offstage the Nanny is singing as she rocks the baby. Enter Masha and Vershinin. As they talk the maid lights the lamp and candles.*)

MASHA: I don't know. (*Pause.*) I don't know. Of course a lot depends on what you're accustomed to. I know after Father died it took us a long time to get used to not having the orderlies around. It's not only what you're accustomed to, though, it just happens that the more respectable or honorable, the more cultivated people in town are with the Army. At least here – maybe it's different somewhere else.

VERSHININ: I'd like some tea; I'm thirsty.

MASHA: (*Glances at her watch.*) They'll bring it soon. When they married me off I was only eighteen. I was completely daunted by my husband, because he was a teacher and I'd only just finished school. I thought he was incredibly bright, scholarly, important. Which is no longer the case, unfortunately.

VERSHININ: Well . . . yes.

MASHA: I'm not talking about my husband, though, I'm used to him. But most civilians are so coarse and unfriendly. They've been brought up so badly; I really can't stand that. Their behavior is insulting; it's painful to see people so uncaring. Of course when I'm with my husband's colleagues, all those teachers, I'm simply in pain.

VERSHININ: Yes, well, as far as I'm concerned, in this town at least, it's all the same: civilian or Army, they're equally uninteresting. Listen to any educated man in town, Army or civilian, and he's sick of his wife, sick of his house, sick of his estate, sick of his horses . . . The Russian thinks on a uniquely high plane, but why in God's name does he live on one so low? Why is that?

MASHA: Why?

VERSHININ: Why is he sick of his children and sick of his wife, and why are his wife and children sick of him?

MASHA: You're in a truly dreadful mood today.

VERSHININ: Maybe I am. I didn't have lunch, I haven't eaten anything since breakfast. One of the girls wasn't feeling well this morning and that always worries me. I suppose I have a bad conscience about giving them such a stepmother. Oh! If you could have seen her today! What a vacuum! We started fighting at seven o'clock this morning, finally at nine I slammed the door and got out. (*Pause.*) I never talk about it; it's strange, but you're the only one I can complain to. (*Kisses her hand.*) I don't want to make you angry; I don't have anyone but you . . . no one, no one. . .

MASHA: Listen to the noise in the stove. Just before father died the chimney moaned like that.

VERSHININ: Are you superstitious?

MASHA: Yes.

VERSHININ: That surprises me. (*Kisses her hand.*) You're a marvelous, wonderful woman. Marvelous, wonderful! It's dark here, but I can see your eyes shining.

MASHA: (*Moving to another chair.*) There's more light here.

VERSHININ: I love, love, love . . . I love your eyes, the way you move; I dream about them. Marvelous, wonderful woman!

MASHA: (*Laughing quietly.*) For some reason it makes me laugh when you talk like that, but really it terrifies me. Please don't say anything more. (*In a low voice.*) Well, no – go on, I don't care. (*Covers her face with her hands.*) I don't care. Someone's coming, change the subject. (*Enter Tuzenbach and Irina through the drawing room.*)

TUZENBACH: I may have three last names but I'm as Russian Orthodox as anyone, in spite of the Baron Tuzenbach-Krone-Altschauer. The only German left in me is in the persistence and stubbornness with which I bore you. Walking you home every night.

IRINA: I can't believe how tired I am.

TUZENBACH: But I'll come to the telegraph office every day and walk you home; ten, twenty years, until you drive me away. (*Seeing Masha and Vershinin.*) Is that you? Hello.

IRINA: I'm home at last. (*To Masha.*) Just before I got off work some woman came into the office to wire her brother in Saratov to tell him that her son had just died. Only she couldn't remember his address, so she had to send it without an address. Just to Saratov. She was crying and I was rude to her for no reason at all; I just told her, I don't have time for this. It was so stupid. Are the Revelers coming tonight?

MASHA: Yes.

IRINA: (*Sits down in an armchair.*) I have to sit down. I can't believe how tired I am.

TUZENBACH: You come home from work looking like some forlorn little waif.

IRINA: (*Pause.*) I can't believe how tired I am. No, I am not in love with the telegraph office. Not in love.

MASHA: You've lost weight. (*Whistles.*) It makes you look younger. Your face looks like a little boy's.

TUZENBACH: It's the haircut.

IRINA: I have to find something else to do. This isn't for me. Everything I'd wanted, everything I dreamed about is exactly what this job doesn't have. There's no poetry in it; just drudgery. (*Someone pounds on the floor.*) The doctor's banging on the floor. (*To Tuzenbach.*) Bang back at him, would you, I don't have the strength . . . I can't believe how tired I am. (*Tuzenbach knocks on the floor.*) He'll be up here in a minute. We've got to do something. Andrei and the doctor went to the club and lost again last night. They say Andrei lost two hundred rubles.

MASHA: (*Indifferently.*) Too late to do anything now.

IRINA: He lost two weeks ago, he lost in December. If he'd just hurry up and lose it all maybe we could get out of here. There's not a night I don't dream about Moscow. Lord, God, I'm acting like a crazy person. (*Laughs.*) We're not going 'til June. Before that, that still leaves, what – all of February, March, April, May, almost half a year.

MASHA: As long as Natasha doesn't find out he's been losing.

IRINA: I don't imagine she'd care one way or the other. (*Chebutykin, who has just got out of bed – he has been reading since lunch – enters the drawing room and combs his beard, he sits down at the table and takes a newspaper from his pocket.*)

MASHA: There he is. Has he paid his rent?

IRINA: (*Laughing.*) No. Not a kopek for the last eight months. He's obviously forgot about it.

MASHA: (*Laughs.*) He sits there with such importance. (*They all laugh.*)

IRINA: (*Pause.*) Why are you so quiet, Aleksandr Ignatych?

VERSHININ: I don't know. I was hoping to get some tea. Half my life for a glass of tea! I haven't had a thing since breakfast.

CHEBUTYKIN: Irina Sergeevna.

IRINA: What?

CHEBUTYKIN: You're going to have to come here. *Venez ici.* (*Irina goes to sit down at the table.*) I can't get along without you. (*Irina lays out cards for a game of solitaire.*)

VERSHININ: All right, then, if we're not going to have tea, at least let's talk about something.

TUZENBACH: What about?

VERSHININ: What about? Let's try to envision, for instance, what life might be like three or four hundred years from now. After we're gone.

TUZENBACH: Well, after we've gone people'll be flying in balloons. The cut of their jackets will be different, they might even discover a sixth sense and develop that, but I don't imagine life will have changed that much. Life will still be hard: half enigmatic, half wonderful. Even a thousand years from now people'll still be complaining that it's a tough life. But they'll be just as terrified and reluctant to let go of it as we are.

VERSHININ: (*After some thought.*) How do I want to say this? I think that everything changes, imperceptibly; and even though we can't see it, it's changing now, right in front of our eyes. After two hundred or three hundred years, or a thousand – how long it takes is immaterial – there'll be a life where people are happy. We won't see it, of course, but we have to strive toward that goal, sacrifice for it. That's the purpose of our lives, and the only happiness we can expect is in the satisfaction of knowing we had a hand in creating that new life. (*Masha laughs quietly.*)

TUZENBACH: What's funny?

MASHA: I don't know, I've been laughing all day, since this morning.

VERSHININ: I went to the same school you went to; I didn't go on to the Academy. I read a lot, but since I had no idea what I was supposed to read, I'm sure I read all the wrong things. But the longer I live the more I want to know. I'm getting grey, I'm almost an old man already, and I still know so little – oh, so little. But the thing that's most important for us to know, that I know; I know that well. Oh, how I'd like to have some way to prove to you that our life has nothing to do with being happy. We're not supposed to be happy. We won't ever be. We're supposed to break the way, and happiness – that's for some future generation. (*Pause.*) Not for me, but at least for my children's children. (*Fedotik and Rodez appear in the drawing room. They sit down and hum quietly while playing the guitar.*)

TUZENBACH: You make it sound as though we shouldn't even dream about being happy, but what if I am happy?

VERSHININ: You're not.

TUZENBACH: (*Throwing up his hands and laughing.*) Obviously we're not understanding each other. I'm going to have to make an argument here. (*Masha laughs softly.*) Laugh! (*Holds up a finger to her.*) Go on, laugh! (*To Vershinin.*) After two hundred, after three hundred, after a million years, life is still going to be what it's always been. It doesn't change, life is perpetual, it follows its own laws that are none of our business, or, in any case, that we'll never fathom. Migrating birds, cranes for example, fly and fly, and whatever thoughts, great or small, that might wander into their heads, they'll still fly and not know why they fly or what they fly for. They just fly and fly, and they'll keep on flying no matter how many philosophers appear among them; and fine, let them philosophize as long as they like, as long as they keep on flying . . .

MASHA: Still, what does it mean?

TUZENBACH: Mean. It's snowing out. What does that mean?

MASHA: I feel we have to believe in something, or we have to try to believe, or our life is empty . . . empty . . . To live and not know why the cranes are flying, why children are born, why there are stars in the sky; I either know who I am and what I'm living for, or it's all just a meaningless flim-flam.

VERSHININ: (*Pause.*) Still, it's too bad we're not young anymore.

MASHA: Gogol said: "My dear friends, it's a depressive world."

TUZENBACH: And I say, my dear friends, it's laborious arguing with you and I'm going to give up on you.

CHEBUTYKIN: (*Reading paper.*) Balzac was married in Berdichev. (*Irina hums softly.*) Well, make a note. Balzac was married in Berdichev. (*Continues reading.*)

IRINA: (*Laying out the cards for a game of solitaire; thoughtfully.*) Balzac was married in Berdichev.

TUZENBACH: Did you hear, Maria Sergeevna? It's all settled. I've resigned my commission.

MASHA: Yes, I heard. And I don't see anything good about it. I don't like civilians.

TUZENBACH: It's all the same . . . (*Stands up.*) I'm not even good-looking, what kind of soldier is that? Oh, well, it's all the same anyway. I'll work. Just one day in my life I'd like to work so hard and come home so exhausted that I'd fall into bed and sleep. (*Walking into the drawing room.*) If nothing else, workers get a good night's sleep.

FEDOTIK: (*To Irina.*) Today, I went to Moscow Street, to Pyzikov's, and got you a set of colored pencils. And this pen knife.

IRINA: You treat me like a little child; I'm an adult. (*Takes the pencils and pen knife, joyfully.*) Oh, they're beautiful!

FEDOTIK: I bought a knife for myself, too . . . Here, see . . . there's a blade, that's another blade, three, this is to clean your ears, a little scissors, a nail file . . .

RODEZ: (*Loudly.*) Doctor, how old are you?

CHEBUTYKIN: Me? Thirty-two. (*Laughter.*)

FEDOTIK: Let me show you another game of solitaire . . . (*Lays cards out . . . The samovar is brought in. Anfisa attends to it. A moment later Natasha arrives and also busies herself at the table. Solyony arrives, greets everyone and sits down at the table.*)

VERSHININ: What a wind.

MASHA: I know. I'm sick of winter. I've forgot what summer is.

IRINA: It's going to work out. We're going to Moscow.

FEDOTIK: No, it's not going to work. See, the eight's on top of the two of spades. (*Laughs.*) So I guess that means you're not going to Moscow.

CHEBUTYKIN: (*Reading paper.*) Tzitzibar. Has an epidemic of smallpox.

ANFISA: (*Going to Masha.*) Masha, tea's ready, come to the table. (*To*

Vershinin.) Your excellency . . . please . . . excuse me . . . I forgot your name.

MASHA: Bring it in here, Nanny. I'm not going there.

IRINA: Nanny!

ANFISA: Coming.

NATASHA: (*To Solyony.*) Little babies understand everything. I said, "Hi there, Bobik. Hi, there, my darling," and he looked at me in that way you knew he'd understood. You think I'm only saying that because I'm his mother, but not at all! Really, he's an extraordinary child.

SOLYONY: If that child were mine I'd fry him in a skillet and eat him. (*Walks with his glass into the parlor and sits down in a corner.*)

NATASHA: (*Covering her face.*) And you're a coarse, ill-bred man!

MASHA: Someone who's happy wouldn't even notice if it was summer now or winter. I think if I were in Moscow I'd be absolutely indifferent to the weather.

VERSHININ: I just read a diary one of the French ministers kept while he was in prison. He'd been involved in the Panama scandal. He wrote about how delighted he was with the birds he saw from his prison window . . . that he'd paid no attention to when he was a minister. Now that he's out, of course, he doesn't notice the birds any more than he did before he went to jail. And you won't notice Moscow when you live there again. There's no happiness for us. It doesn't exist. It's just something we wish for.

TUZENBACH: (*Picking up a box from the table.*) Where's the candy?

IRINA: Solyony ate it.

TUZENBACH: All of it?

ANFISA: (*Serving tea.*) There's a letter for you, sir.

VERSHININ: For me? (*Takes it.*) From my daughter. (*Reads the letter.*) Oh, of course . . . I, excuse me, Maria Sergeevna, I'll sneak out. I can't have tea. (*Stands up agitated.*) The same old story . . .

MASHA: What is it? It's no secret, surely?

VERSHININ: (*Quietly.*) My wife's taken poison again. I have to go. I'll try to leave unnoticed. This is all terribly unpleasant. (*Kisses Masha's hands.*) My dear, fine, wonderful, woman . . . I'll sneak out this way . . . (*Leaves.*)

ANFISA: Where's he off to? He's an odd one, I've just got tea served.

MASHA: Leave me alone! Stop hovering, I don't have a minute's peace . . . (*Walks with her cup to the table.*) I'm sick of you, you old nag.

ANFISA: I didn't mean to upset you, darling.

ANDREI'S VOICE: (*Off.*) Anfisa!

ANFISA: (*Mocking.*) "Anfisa," and there he sits. (*Goes out.*)

MASHA: (*In the drawing room by the table, angrily.*) Make some room, you take up the whole table. (*Jumbles up the cards.*) Lolling over year cards. Drink your tea!

IRINA: Masha, you're behaving abominably.

MASHA: So I'm behaving abominably; so don't talk to me. Don't bother me.

CHEBUTYKIN: (*Laughing.*) Don't bother her. Don't bother . . .

Act II

MASHA: You're sixty years old, you act like a baby; no one knows what the hell you're drivelling about.

NATASHA: (*Sighs.*) Masha, sweetheart, why do you employ such profanity in your conversation? With your looks you could move in the most fashionable circles in town; I mean it, you could be just charming if you'd forego those naughty words. *Je vous prie pardonnez moi, Marie, mais vous avez des manieres un peu grossieres.* [I beg you to excuse me, Marie, but you are slightly uncouth.]

TUZENBACH: (*Trying to keep from laughing.*) Pass me . . . pass me . . . I believe that's Cognac . . .

NATASHA: *Il parait, que mon Bobik deja ne dort pas el il est . . .* [It seems my Bobik is no longer asleep and is . . .] wide awake. He isn't feeling well today. I'll go check on him. Excuse me. (*Exits.*)

IRINA: Where did Vershinin go?

MASHA: Home. His wife is acting weirdly again.

TUZENBACH: (*Walking toward Solyony with a decanter of Cognac.*) You're sitting over here all by yourself. Thinking about something, you don't even know what. Let's make up. Let's have a Cognac. (*They drink.*) I suppose I'll have to play the piano all night. Probably play nothing but a lot of tripe. Oh, well . . .

SOLYONY: How can we make up? We haven't quarreled.

TUZENBACH: You keep making me feel something's happened between us. You have to admit you're very strange.

SOLYONY: (*Reciting.*) "Strange I be, but who is not? Withhold thy wrath, *Aleko!*" [Strange I be . . . *]

---

*from *Woe from Wit* by A.S. Griboedov. The hero is surrounded by hypocritical Moscow society. Aleko, Pushkin's hero, is a cuckold husband who kills his wife and her lover.

TUZENBACH: How'd Aleko get in there?

SOLYONY: (*Pause.*) When I'm with someone, just the two of us, I'm like anyone else, but gatherings depress me, they make me uncomfortable. I talk nothing but a lot of tripe. But I think I'm more honest and generous that most. And I can prove it.

TUZENBACH: You're always trying to annoy me if there's anyone around; I get so angry with you. But I like you anyway. Oh, well, if nothing else tonight, at least I'm going to get drunk. *Vwepem!* [Let's drink]

SOLYONY: *Vwepem!* (*They drink.*) I have nothing against you, personally, Baron. I have a temperament like Lermontov . . . (*Quietly.*) Apparently I look something like Lermontov . . . at least that's what people say. (*Takes a bottle of cologne from his pocket, sprinkles some on his hands.*)

TUZENBACH: I've resigned my commission. Enough is enough. I've been vacillating for five years, now it's over with. I'm going to get a job.

SOLYONY: (*Reciting.*) "Withhold thy wrath, *Aleko* . . . Forget, forget thy dreams . . . " (*As they speak Andrei enters quietly with a book, sits by the candle.*)

TUZENBACH: I'm going to get a job.

CHEBUTYKIN: (*Walking into the parlor with Irina.*) And we were treated to a genuine Caucasian meal. Onion soup, and the meat course was a chekhartma.

SOLYONY: Cheremsha isn't meat, it's a vegetable – like a leek.

CHEBUTYKIN: I'm afraid not, my friend, chekhartma certainly isn't a leek. It's a kind of roast mutton.

SOLYONY: And I tell you cheremsha is a leek.

Act II

CHEBUTYKIN: And I tell you chekhartma is mutton.

SOLYONY: And I tell you cheremsha is a leek.

CHEBUTYKIN: I'm not going to argue with you. You've never been in The Caucasus, you've never eaten chekhartma in your life.

SOLYONY: I've never eaten cheremsha because I hate it. It stinks like garlic.

ANDREI: (*Imploring.*) Enough, gentlemen, please.

TUZENBACH: When are the Revelers coming?

IRINA: They said about nine. They're due now.

TUZENBACH: (*Embracing Andrei. Singing.*) Oh you bower, my dear bower / Oh my bower, newly made;*

ANDREI: (*Dancing and singing.*) Bower, carved from new maple / Of a light and pretty shade.

CHEBUTYKIN: (*Dancing.*) And if only I could walk there, / By my bower late at night; / With my lover holding my hand / In her own hand pressing tight. (*Laughter.*)

TUZENBACH: (*Kissing Andrei.*) Damnit all, Andryusha, have a drink. Let's drink to our friendship. And I'm coming to Moscow with you, Andryusha. To the University.

SOLYONY: Which one?

ANDREI: There's only one university in Moscow.

SOLYONY: And I tell you there are two.

---

*Traditional folk song usually translated "My Porch of Maplewood"

ANDREI: Why don't we make it three. The more the merrier.

SOLYONY: There are two universities in Moscow. (*Sounds of people protesting, others telling them to be quiet.*) There are two universities in Moscow. The old one and the new one. But if you don't want to listen to me; if you can't take the truth, then I'll be still. I'll go as far as to remove myself to another room. (*Leaves through one of the doors.*)

TUZENBACH: Bravo, bravo! (*Laughs.*) All right, everyone, I know – go on, I'll sit down and play. Solyony is funny. (*Sits at the piano, plays a waltz.*)

MASHA: (*Dancing the waltz by herself.*) The baron is drunk, the baron is drunk, the baron is drunk!

NATASHA: (*Enters, goes to Chebutykin.*) Ivan Romanych! (*Talks to Chebutykin, then quietly leaves. Chebutykin touches Tuzenbach on the shoulder and whispers to him.*)

IRINA: What's wrong?

CHEBUTYKIN: Time to go. Goodbye.

TUZENBACH: Good night. Time to go.

IRINA: Wait a minute . . . what about the Revelers?

ANDREI: (*Embarrassed.*) They're not coming. Not tonight, darling, Natasha says Bobik isn't feeling well, so . . . well, I don't know anything about it, and I certainly don't care.

IRINA: (*Shrugging.*) Bobik's not feeling well!

MASHA: Too bad the season's so short, but what the hell! Since they're driving us away, I suppose what we do is leave. (*To Irina.*) Bobik isn't the one who's sick, it's she. Up here. (*Taps her head.*) Common bitch. (*Andrei goes out of the door R. to his room. Chebutykin goes after him. In the drawing room everyone is saying goodbye.*)

FEDOTIK: That's a shame. I thought we'd be here all night; but if the boy's sick . . . I'll bring him something to play with tomorrow.

RODEZ: (*Loudly.*) I thought we were going to dance all night; I took a nap. It's only nine o'clock.

MASHA: Let's move this out into the street, we'll decide where we're going out there. (*Voices are heard saying goodbye, good night! The merry laughter of Tuzenbach is heard. Everyone leaves. Anfisa and the maid are cleaning the table, putting out the candles. The nanny can be heard singing. Andrei, wearing a coat and hat, comes in quietly with Chebutykin.*)

CHEBUTYKIN: I never found the time to get married; for one thing, life just flashed by me with the speed of light. Then, I was so much in love with your mother, and she was married . . .

ANDREI: There's no good reason to get married. No reason. It's too boring.

CHEBUTYKIN: Oh, I'm sure, but let me tell you the alternative is a very lonely proposition, and you can talk all you like, my friend, but it's hell being lonely. Actually, though, really, who gives a damn?

ANDREI: Hurry up.

CHEBUTYKIN: We have time, there's no rush.

ANDREI: My wife might not let me go.

CHEBUTYKIN: Ah . . .

ANDREI: I'm not going to play, I'll just sit and watch. I don't feel that well. What do you do for shortness of breath, Doctor?

CHEBUTYKIN: Don't ask me, I don't know. Who remembers?

ANDREI: Let's go through the kitchen. (*The doorbell rings; rings again. The sound of voices, laughter. They leave.*)

IRINA: (*Entering.*) Who's there?

ANFISA: (*Whisper.*) The Revelers!

IRINA: Tell them nobody's home, Nanny. Say we're sorry. (*Anfisa leaves. Irina, preoccupied, paces the floor, upset. Enter Solyony.*)

SOLYONY: (*Confused.*) No one's here. Where'd they all go?

IRINA: They went home.

SOLYONY: That's odd. You're here by yourself?

IRINA: Yes, I'm here by myself. (*Pause.*) Goodbye.

SOLYONY: I've been finding it very difficult to behave with any kind of restraint lately; I've been tactless. But you're not like they are, you're above that; you see past all that, to what's true; what's really there. You have a purity . . . I think you're the only one who's capable of understanding me. The depth of my love for you staggers me; I love you with an infinite –

IRINA: Goodbye. Go away.

SOLYONY: I couldn't live without you. (*Following her.*) Oh, my blessings! (*Through tears.*) Oh, happiness! Those languid, marvelous, dazzling eyes; no other woman on earth has eyes like that.

IRINA: (*Coldly.*) Just stop it, Vasily Vasilych!

SOLYONY: I tell you that I love you for the first time in my life and you treat me like I wasn't on earth; like I was on some other planet.

(*Wipes his forehead.*) Well, forget it. I know I can't force myself on you. but I will not tolerate anyone else having you. I will not. I swear to you by all I hold holy if there's anyone else, I'll kill him . . . Oh, God, you're wonderful! (*Natasha passes by with a candle.*)

NATASHA: (*After peering into one door, then another, she walks past the door leading to her husband's room.*) Andrei's here; well, let him read. Solyony! Forgive me, I didn't realize you were here. I'm not dressed for company.

SOLYONY: Who cares? Goodbye. (*He goes out.*)

NATASHA: (*To Irina.*) You're tired, aren't you, dear, you poor thing. (*Kisses her.*) You should have gone to bed hours ago.

IRINA: Did Bobik get to sleep?

NATASHA: He went to sleep, but he's so restless. Oh, darling, I've been wanting to talk to you, but you're so rarely home, or I never seem to have the time. Bobik's nursery is so cold and damp. Your room's perfect for a baby. Could you be a dear and move in with Olga for a while?

IRINA: (*Not understanding.*) Where? (*Offstage, the sound of a troika with bells, driving up to the house.*)

NATASHA: You and Olga can share her room for a while and Bobik can have your room. He's such a sweetie. I told him today, "Bobik, you're my baby. You're mine." And he looked up at me with those eyesies of his. (*Doorbell rings.*) That's Olga. She's so late. (*The maid comes to Natasha and whispers something in her ear.*) Protopopov? What a character. Protopopov's come to take me for a ride in his troika. (*Laughs.*) Men are the most peculiar . . . (*Doorbell rings.*) There's someone else. I guess I could go for a sleigh ride; a short one, no more than a quarter of an hour. (*To maid.*) Tell him in a minute. (*Doorbell rings.*) The doorbell is ringing! That'll be Olga. (*She exits. The maid runs out. Irina sits, preoccupied. Enter Kulygin and Olga followed by Vershinin.*)

KULYGIN: What happened? They said we were having a party.

VERSHININ: That's odd, I just left half an hour ago, they were expecting the Revelers.

IRINA: Everyone's gone.

KULYGIN: Masha left? Where'd she go? And what's Protopopov doing downstairs in a troika? Whom's he waiting for?

IRINA: Don't ask questions . . I can't believe how tired I am.

KULYGIN: Don't be capricious.

OLGA: The meeting just now broke up. I'm exhausted. The principal was ill, I had to take her place. Oh, my head, my head is killing me; my head . . . (*Sits.*) Andrei lost two hundred rubles last night playing cards . . . it's all over town.

KULYGIN: The meeting did me in, too. (*Sits.*)

VERSHININ: My wife decided it was time to put another scare into me; very nearly succeeded in poisoning herself. I'm glad to report everything's back to normal, finally, and I can relax. So, we'll have to leave? Well, fine, then, Fyodor Illich, let's go out somewhere! I couldn't stay at home if I wanted to. Not if I wanted to . . . let's go out.

KULYGIN: I'm too tired to go out, I couldn't. (*Gets up.*) I'm tired. My wife's gone home?

IRINA: Probably.

KULYGIN: (*Kisses Irina's hand.*) Goodbye. We have the whole weekend to rest up. All the best. (*Going out.*) I'd like to have had some tea. I was hoping to spend the evening with a pleasant group of people, but – *O, fallacem hominum spem!* [Oh, the deceit of human hope!] Always use the accusative case in exclamations . . .

VERSHININ: Well, I'll go by myself then. (*Goes out with Kulygin, whistling.*)

OLGA: My head is killing me. Oh, my head . . . Andrei lost . . . The whole town's talking . . . I've got to lie down. (*Starts to leave.*) I'm off tomorrow; God, that's wonderful. I'm off all weekend. My head is killing me . . . oh, my head . . . (*Leaves.*)

IRINA: (*Alone.*) Everyone's gone. No one's here. (*Outside the sound of an accordion is heard. Nanny is singing a song. Natasha walks across the drawing room in a fur coat and hat with the maid following.*)

NATASHA: I'll be back in half an hour. I'm just going for a short little ride. (*Leaves.*)

IRINA: (*Left alone, with longing.*) To Moscow! To Moscow! To Moscow!

CURTAIN

Act Three

Olga and Irina's room. To the L. and R. are beds hidden by screens.
It is between two and three a.m. Offstage the tocsin is sounding. A
fire has broken out sometime before. It is obvious no one in the
house has been to bed. Masha is on the sofa in the usual black dress.
Enter Olga and Anfisa.

ANFISA: They're all huddled up down in the hall; I said come upstairs, it's
no good sitting down here bawling your eyes out. They just keep on
yelling, "Oh, we've lost our daddy. Oh. God, what if he burned up
in the fire!" What nonsense! And there's another pack of them out in
the yard . . . half undressed.

OLGA: (*Taking a dress from the wardrobe.*) Here, take this grey one
. . . and this . . . the blouse too . . . and this skirt . . . look what
you're doing, Nanny . . . What is all this stuff? My God! Kirsanov
Lane burned to the ground . . . here take this too. (*Throws the clothes
into Anfisa's arms.*) The Vershinin's must have been scared to death.
Their house came within inches of being burned. We'll have to take
them in tonight, we can't let them go home . . . Poor Fedotik lost
everything, everything he had was burned; nothing's left at all.

ANFISA: You're going to have to call Ferapont, Oliushka, I can't take all
this.

OLGA: (*Rings.*) I can ring all I like, no one will answer. (*Calling out the
door.*) Whoever's down there, come up here. (*Through the open door
you can see a window, red from the glow. You can hear the fire brigade
driving past the house.*) This is just ghastly! It's also just exhausting!
(*Enter Ferapont.*) Here, take this down to the Kolotilin girls, they're
down in the foyer . . . and give them this.

FERAPONT: I hear you. This is just like when Moscow burned in eighteen
twelve. Lord, God Almighty, was the French flabber-gasted.

OLGA: Leave! Go!

FERAPONT: I hear you. (*Exits.*)

OLGA: Nanny, darling, just give it all away. We don't need it, give it away . . . I'm exhausted, I can barely stand on my feet . . . we can't let the Vershinins go home. The girls can sleep in the living room, Colonel Vershinin can stay down with the baron . . . Fedotik can go in with the baron, too . . . or he can have the drawing room. The doctor – you'd think he'd done it on purpose – is stinking drunk, he couldn't take anyone if he wanted. We can put Vershinin's wife in the living room, too.

ANFISA: (*Imploring.*) Olya, baby, don't kick me out. Don't kick me out.

OLGA: What? What are you talking about? Nobody's going to kick you out.

ANFISA: (*Putting her hand on Olga's breast.*) My baby, my treasure, I work hard, I do everything I can, but I can't go on forever; I'll get feeble and they'll say, let her go! But where can I go? Where? I'm eighty years old; I'm in my eighty-second year.

OLGA: Sit down, Nanny . . . you're exhausted, darling. (*Helps her to sit.*) Look how pale . . . rest a minute. (*Natasha enters.*)

NATASHA: They're talking about getting together an emergency committee for the people who've lost their homes . . . which is only right, don't you think? It's the obligation of the wealthy to help those who are less fortunate – usually. Bobik and little Sophia slept right through everything just as if nothing had happened. There're people everywhere. Everywhere you turn the house is full of them. And the flu's been going around town, I hope the children don't catch something.

OLGA: (*Not listening to her.*) You can't see the fire from here; at least it's quiet.

NATASHA: Yes . . . I must look a mess. (*Looking in mirror.*) Someone said

I'd put on weight . . . and it's not true. Not at all. Masha's sleeping; I'm glad someone can, she was exhausted, poor darling. (*Seeing Anfisa, coldly.*) What do you mean sitting down in front of me! Get up! Get out! (*Anfisa goes. Pause.*) It's beyond me why you hang onto that old woman.

OLGA: (*Struck dumb.*) Excuse me, but it's also beyond me why . . .

NATASHA: She's absolutely useless. The woman's about as useful in the house as a field hand; she should be put out to pasture . . . that's what you get for being so easy on everyone. I like a house to be run with some semblance of order, at least; you can't have people doing nothing. (*Strokes her cheek.*) You poor darling, you're tired! We have a tired principal. When my little Sophia gets big enough to go to school, I'm going to be terrified of you.

OLGA: I'm not going to be the new principal.

NATASHA: You're the one they'll pick, Olechka; that's been taken care of.

OLGA: I'll decline . . . I can't . . . I don't have the strength for it. (*Drinks some water.*) You were so cruel to Nanny just now . . . I'm sorry, I can't bear that . . . Everything went black.

NATASHA: (*Upset.*) I'm sorry, Olya, forgive me . . . I don't want to upset you. (*Masha stands up, takes a pillow and goes out angrily.*)

OLGA: Understand, dear . . . maybe we were reared strangely, but I can't bear that sort of behavior. It's very depressing for me to see people treated that way. It makes me physically ill; I simply lose heart . . .

NATASHA: I'm sorry, I'm sorry. (*Kisses her.*)

OLGA: Anything, the slightest harshness, tactlessness, an indelicately spoken word, upsets me.

NATASHA: I know; you're right, I'm always talking when I shouldn't; but you know as well as I do how much better off she'd be in the country.

OLGA: She's been with us for thirty years.

NATASHA: I know, only she can't work anymore! Either I don't understand you, or you aren't even trying to understand me. She is just no longer capable of working. What she's capable of doing is sitting and sleeping.

OLGA: Then let her sit!

NATASHA: (*With surprise.*) How can I let her sit? The woman works for us! (*Through tears.*) I do not understand you, Olya, I have a nanny, I have a wet nurse, we have a cook, we have a maid . . . what do we need that broken-down old woman for? For what? (*Offstage the tocsin sounds.*)

OLGA: I've aged ten years tonight.

NATASHA: We have to get something straight, Olya. You're at the school, I'm home. Your job is teaching, mine is running the house. And if I say something about the help, I know what I'm talking about. I know what I am talk! – ing! A! – bout! and that witch, that thief had better be out of here tomorrow . . . (*Stamps her foot.*) That hag! How dare something annoy me! How dare it! (*Getting control of herself.*) Really, if you don't move your things to one of the rooms downstairs, we're just going to be quarreling all the time. This is horrible. (*Enter Kulygin.*)

KULYGIN: Where's Masha? It's time we were getting home. They say the fire's dying down. (*Stretches.*) Even with all that wind only one block burned; it looked for a while like the whole town would go. (*Sits down.*) I'm exhausted. My darling Olechka, I've always thought if I hadn't married Masha, I'd have married you, Olechka; you're so good . . . Oh, I'm worn out. (*Listens attentively.*)

OLGA: What is it?

KULYGIN: The doctor's gone on a spree. Conveniently. He's got himself hopelessly drunk. I don't doubt on purpose. (*Stands up.*) I thought he was coming up. You hear anything? Yes, he is. (*Laughs.*) He's really something . . . I'll get out of sight. (*Goes behind wardrobe and stands in the corner.*) What a rascal.

OLGA: Getting himself in that condition after being so good for two years. (*Walks with Natasha to the back of the room. Chebutykin enters, walks straight, as if sober, goes through the room, then stops, looks, walks up to the washstand and begins to wash his hands.*)

CHEBUTYKIN: (*Morosely.*) To hell with all of them. Blast 'em to hell. They think I'm a doctor, they think I should be able to heal the world. I don't know a damn thing; whatever I knew I forgot, remember nothing, absolutely nothing. (*Olga and Natasha leave without his noticing.*) To hell with all of them. Treated a woman from Zasyp last Wednesday. And she died. Thanks to me she's dead. I might have known something twenty-five years ago, but who remembers any of it now. Nothing. Maybe I'm not a man, maybe I just make believe that I have arms and legs and a head. Maybe I don't exist at all, I just imagine I walk and eat and sleep. (*Cries.*) Oh, God, if I didn't exist! (*Stops crying, sullenly.*) Who the hell knows. Day before yesterday they were all talking about Shakespeare and Voltaire at the club. I never read them, never read a word of them; but I sat there and nodded and smiled knowingly – and so did all the rest of them. Vulgar! Lies! Then I thought about the woman I'd murdered on Wednesday . . . it all came back . . . that what heart I had has become so twisted and obscene and vile . . . that I went out and got drunk. (*Enter Irina, Vershinin and Tuzenbach. Tuzenbach is wearing a new and fashionable suit.*)

IRINA: We can sit in here; no one will come in.

VERSHININ: If it hadn't been for the troops the whole town would have gone. (*Rubs his hands with pleasure.*) Good men! Pure gold. What fine men they are!

KULYGIN: (*Going to them.*) What time do you have, my friends?

TUZENBACH: Nearly four. It's getting light out.

IRINA: They're all down in the drawing room. That Solyony of yours is down there . . . No one's even thinking about leaving. (*To Chebutykin.*) You should go to bed, doctor.

CHEBUTYKIN: Nothing, thank you. (*Combs his beard.*)

KULYGIN: (*Laughing.*) You're feeling no pain, doctor. (*Claps him on the shoulder.*) Good boy. *In vino veritas,* as the ancients tell us.

TUZENBACH: They're asking me to organize a concert to aid some of the people who were burned out.

IRINA: Fine, only who can you get?

TUZENBACH: I think we might arrange a very nice concert if they're really interested. Masha plays the piano like an angel.

KULYGIN: Like an angel.

IRINA: She's out of practice; she hasn't played in three years . . . four.

TUZENBACH: Not a soul in this town has any understanding of music at all, but I do. I do understand music and believe me, Masha is a brilliant pianist, she's tremendously gifted.

KULYGIN: I agree completely, Baron. I love Masha very much. She's glorious.

TUZENBACH: To have the ability to play so well and know that no one understands it.

KULYGIN: (*Sighing.*) Yes . . . But would it be quite right for her to play in public? (*Pause.*) I, well, don't know anything about it. It might be perfectly acceptable. I must tell you, though, that our principal, though he's a good man, very good actually, extremely intelligent, he does have definite views. Of course, it'd be none of his business. But, if you'd like, I can certainly have a word with him. (*Chebutykin picks up a porcelain clock and examines it.*)

VERSHININ: That fire's got me filthy. I look like nothing on earth. (*Pause.*) Talk has it our brigade might be transferred out of here before long. Some say to Poland, some were saying Siberia.

TUZENBACH: That's what I hear, but I can't believe it. The town would be completely deserted.

IRINA: Then I'm glad we're leaving too.

CHEBUTYKIN: (*Drops the clock, which breaks.*) Smashed to smithereens . . . (*Pause. Everyone is upset and embarrassed.*)

KULYGIN: (*Picking up the pieces.*) Ivan Romanych, Ivan Romanych! To break a valuable piece like that. Zero minus for deportment!

IRINA: That was Mama's clock.

CHEBUTYKIN: Why not? . . . If it's your mama's, it's your mama's. Maybe I didn't break it, it only looks like it's broken. Maybe it only looks like we're here, and we're really not here at all. What do I know? Who knows anything? (*Stops at the door.*) What are you looking at me for? Natasha's having an affair with Protopopov and you look right past that . . . You sit there and are blind to the fact that Natasha is having an affair with Protopopov . . . (*Sings.*) "How do you like that little tidbit?" (*Goes out.*)

VERSHININ: Yes . . . (*Laughs.*) That's certainly very strange! (*Pause.*) I dropped everything when the fire started and ran home as fast as I could. I could see the house was in no real danger, of course, when I got close enough, but my two little girls were standing in the doorway, still in their nightgowns, their mother gone. There was an absolute maelstrom of people, horses running, dogs, and my girls had such a look of alarm, of terror, of supplication, of I don't know what on their faces; a look that would break your heart. I could only think, my God, how much more are these children going to have to go through in their long lives? I grabbed them up and ran and all I could think of, all the way here, was how much more on this earth will these children have to go through? (*The tocsin sounds. Pause.*) By the time I got here, of course, their mother was here already, screaming, furious.(*Masha enters with a pillow and sits down on the sofa.*) I know when my girls were standing there in the doorway, in their nightclothes, in that deafening noise, with the street all red from the fire, I thought this is what it must have been like years ago when the barbarians made surprise forays into our country . . . plundering and burning . . . but really, there's no comparison between now and the way things were then. And with a little more time, some two or three hundred years, people will look back on our lives with the same horror and derision that we look back to those barbarous times. One day everything we have will seem awkward and primitive and unpleasant, strange. Oh, Lord! What a life that's going to be. What a life! (*Laughs.*) I'm sorry, I'm speculating again . . . but let me go on, I'm dying to talk. I'm in a talking mood. (*Pause.*) I think they're all asleep. I still say what a life that's going to be! You can just imagine . . . take people like you: now there may only be three of you in town, but in the next generation they'll be more, then more, and more and the time will come when life will be everything you could wish for it to be. Life will be everything you wish for. And then, when you're very old, people will come along who are even better than you are. (*Laughs.*) I'm in a rare mood today. I want like the devil to live. (*Sings.*) "To love all ages must submit; its pain confers such benefit."

MASHA: Tram-tam-tam . . .

VERSHININ: Tam-tam.

MASHA: Tra-ra-ra?

VERSHININ: Tra-ta-ta. (*Laughs. Enter Fedotik.*)

FEDOTIK: (*Dancing.*) Burned, burned! Everything completely consumed! (*Laughter.*)

IRINA: It's nothing to joke about! Is everything gone?

FEDOTIK: Everything completely! Nothing's left at all. The guitar was consumed, all the photographs consumed, all my letters . . . and a little notebook that I got for you, but that was consumed too. (*Enter Solyony.*)

IRINA: No, absolutely not. Please go, Vasily Vasilych, You can't come in here.

SOLYONY: How come the baron can be here and I can't?

VERSHININ: We really do have to go. How's the fire?

SOLYONY: They say it's burning out. No, I don't understand why the baron can be here and I can't. (*Takes a bottle of cologne and sprays himself.*)

VERSHININ: Tram-tam-tam?

MASHA: Tram-tram.

VERSHININ: (*Laughing, to Solyony.*) Let's go down to the drawing room.

SOLYONY: Very well, then, make a note of it. "This thought I could more pointedly explain, But I fear to do so lest the geese complain." (*Looking at Tuzenbach.*) Chicky, chicky, chicky. (*Goes out with Vershinin and Fedotik.*)

IRINA: That Solyony; the stink he leaves, he might as well've smoked up the room. (*Bewildered.*) The baron's asleep! Baron! Baron!

TUZENBACH: (*Waking.*) I'm too tired . . . The brickyard . . . I'm not talking in my sleep, I'm really going to the brickyard, to work. I've had my interview. (*To Irina, tenderly.*) You're so wonderful, so charming . . . you're so pale you seem to brighten the dark around you like light . . . you're sad, I know you're not happy with the life you have here . . . go away with me, go away with me and we'll work together . . .

MASHA: Nikolai Lvovich, get out of here.

TUZENBACH: (*Laughing.*) You're here? I didn't see you. (*Kisses Irina's hand.*) Goodbye, I'm going to go . . . it's just that I was looking at you and thinking about the Saint's Day party you had . . . it seems forever ago, doesn't it? When you were so vivacious and carefree, and you were talking about how wonderful it would be to work. I thought back then that I'd have such a happy life ahead of me. Where is it? (*Kisses her hand.*) You're crying. You should go to bed. It's getting light out . . . It's morning. If only I could be allowed to give my life for you!

MASHA: Nikolai Lvovich, go away! Really!

TUZENBACH: I'm going. (*He leaves.*)

MASHA: (*Lying down.*) Are you asleep, Fyodor?

KULYGIN: What?

MASHA: You should go home.

KULYGIN: My sweet Masha; my beautiful Masha . . .

IRINA: She's exhausted, let her rest, Fedya . . .

KULYGIN: I'm going right away . . . my good, wonderful wife. My one and only, I love you.

MASHA: (*Angrily.*) *Amo, ama, amat, amamus, amatis, amant!*

KULYGIN: (*Laughing.*) No, she really is astonishing. We've been married seven years, it seems like yesterday. I swear. No, honestly, you're an astonishing woman. I'm content, I'm content, I'm content.

MASHA: I'm fed up; fed up, fed up! (*Sits up, continues talking while seated.*) Also, I can't get it out of my head . . . It's simply infuriating. It's a nail in my skull; I can't be still about it. Andrei's mortgaged the house and his wife's grabbed all the money. And the house isn't even his; it belongs to all four of us! He has to know that if he has any integrity at all.

KULYGIN: What's the point, Masha? Why bother? Your brother's in debt everywhere, leave him alone.

MASHA: I don't care, it's infuriating. (*Lies down.*)

KULYGIN: You and I aren't poor. I work, I have my job at the school, I make a little something from private tutoring. I'm a plain, honest man . . . *Omnia mea mecum porto,* [Everything that is mine, I carry with me,] as they say.

MASHA: I don't want anything; I'm just infuriated by the injustice of it. (*Pause.*) Go on, Fydor.

KULYGIN: (*Kisses her.*) You're tired. Rest for half an hour, I'll wait downstairs. Try to sleep. (*Moves off.*) I'm content, I'm content, I'm content. (*Goes out.*)

IRINA: It's true, though . . . Andrei's fallen completely apart; how that woman's aged him, how she's worn him down to just nothing. He used to be working for his doctorate, now yesterday he was actually bragging about finally being a member of the City Council. Andrei's on the council and Protopopov's chairman . . . the whole town's talking about it, it's a joke; he's the only person in town who doesn't know what's going on; doesn't have eyes in his head. Everyone runs off to the fire tonight, he sits in there by himself, totally unaware. Playing his violin. (*Nervously.*) Oh, it's horrible, horrible, horrible! (*Cries.*) I can't, I can't, I can't stand it anymore! I can't anymore! (*Sobbing loudly.*) I've got to get out of here; get me out of here; I can't anymore! (*Olga enters, tidies up her bedside table.*)

OLGA: (*Frightened.*) What's wrong with you? What's wrong? Dar-ling . . .

IRINA: (*Sobbing.*) Where? Where's it all gone? Where is it? Oh, my God, my God! My mind is a total muddle . . . I can't even remember the Italian for window or ceiling . . . I forget everything, every day I've forgot something else. My life is just slipping away and I'll never, never get it back . . . and we're never going to Moscow, it's as clear as it can be, we're never going to leave here.

OLGA: Darling, darling . . .

IRINA: (*Trying to control herself.*) Oh, I'm miserable . . . I can't work, I can't work, I'm not going to work anymore. Enough, enough! First the telegraph office, now the City Council, and I loathe and despise every piece of work they give me . . . I'm nearly twenty four, I've been working forever and my brain has just atrophied. I've got thin, I've got ugly, I've got old and nothing, nothing, not the least sense of fulfillment, and time is passing and all I know is I'm moving farther away from any good, real life; I'm being drawn farther and farther away from everything I'd hoped for, into some abyss. And why I'm even alive, why I haven't killed myself by now I can't understand.

OLGA: Don't cry, my little girl, don't cry. It kills me to see you cry.

IRINA: I'm not crying, not crying . . . enough . . . Now, there, I'm not crying anymore. Enough . . . enough!

OLGA: Darling, let me tell you as a sister, as a friend. If you'd take my advice you'd marry the baron! (*Irina cries quietly.*) You respect him, you think highly of him. I know he's not dashing maybe, but he's a decent, moral man . . . Women marry because it's their duty to marry, not always for love. At least I'm beginning to think so; I would, even without love. I'd go; it wouldn't matter to me who it was, if he was a decent man. Even someone older.

IRINA: I've always held back, because I kept thinking one day we would go to Moscow; and there my real life would begin . . . I've dreamed of him . . . loved him . . . but it isn't going to happen . . . it won't happen.

OLGA: (*Hugging her.*) Oh, my beautiful darling sister, I really do know what you mean. When Baron Nikolai Lvovich resigned the Army I took one look at him in his bright new street clothes and he was so homely I actually burst into tears . . . He said, "Why are you crying?" I couldn't very well tell him . . . But if God has brought him here to be your bridegroom, it's a very different matter. (*Natasha comes through the door on the right carrying a candle and crosses the stage silently, going through the door, L.*)

MASHA: (*Sitting down.*) I wouldn't be surprised to learn she'd set the fire herself.

OLGA: Masha, you're being silly. You're the silliest one in the family.

MASHA: (*Pause.*) My dear sisters, I want to tell you something. It's on my conscience. I'll confess to you and never mention it again to anyone, ever. I'd better tell you this minute. (*Quietly.*) I've tried to hide it, but I want you to know . . . I can't not say it anyway . . . (*Pause.*) I'm in love, love . . . I love that man . . . you just saw him . . . well, that's it . . . quite simply, I love Vershinin.

OLGA: (*Going behind her screen.*) Stop it. I don't care, I can't hear you.

MASHA: What can I do?! (*Holds her head.*) At first I thought he was ridiculous; then I felt sorry for him . . . then I fell in love. I fell in love with his voice, with the things he said, with his miserable life . . . with his two daughters . . .

OLGA: (*Behind the screen.*) I can't hear you, I don't care. Whatever silliness you're saying, I don't care, because I can't hear you.

MASHA: You're the one who's being silly, Olya. I love him . . . that's my fate; I have to live with it . . . and he loves me . . . I'm not saying it's good, it's horrible. It's not good at all. (*Takes Irina by the hand, pulls her closer.*) Little darling . . . we'll live our lives somehow . . . What happens to people like us? It's so easy when you read about it in a novel; everything's so pat, everything's so clearly laid out for you. And then you fall in love yourself and you realize nobody knows anything about it. They haven't helped you a bit. You have to make your own decisions. So, my darlings, my sisters . . . that's my confession, now I'll be quiet . . . I'm like Gogol's madman . . . silent . . . silent . . . (*Enter Andrei, followed by Ferapont.*)

ANDREI: (*Angrily.*) What do you want? I don't understand.

FERAPONT: I've told you ten times, Andrei Sergevich.

ANDREI: To begin with, I'm not Andrei Sergevich to you, I'm "Sir."

FERAPONT: It's the firemen, sir. They're asking can they drive to the river through the garden? They've been going the long way around – pure punishment.

ANDREI: All right, then, tell them it's all right. (*Ferapont leaves.*) I'm sick of all of them. Where's Olga? (*Olga comes from behind the screen.*) Give me your key to the cupboard, I've lost mine. That little key you have. (*Olga silently gives him the key. Irina goes behind the screen. Pause.*) What an enormous fire! It's dying down, now. Damn that Ferapont. Made me say the most ridiculous . . . "call me sir." (*Pause.*) Are you just not talking to me anymore, Olya? (*Pause.*) It's about time you dropped this absurd behavior and stopped pouting over nothing. Masha's here, Irina's here, good: maybe we can get everything out in the open, once and for all. I want to know what you have against me. What is it?

OLGA: Leave it alone, Andryusha. We can have it out tomorrow. (*Getting agitated.*) What an agonizing night!

ANDREI: (*Extremely confused, embarrassed.*) Don't get upset, I'm asking you as calmly as I can. What do you have against me? Just tell me.

VERSHININ'S VOICE: "Tram-tam-tam!"

MASHA: (*Stands up, loudly.*) Tra-ta-ta! (*Olga.*) Good night, Olya, God be with you. (*Goes behind the screen to kiss Irina.*) Sleep well . . . good night, Andrei. Go away. They're exhausted . . . Have it out tomorrow . . . (*Goes.*)

OLGA: Really, Andryusha, leave it 'til tomorrow . . . (*Goes behind the screen.*) It's bedtime.

ANDREI: I just want to say this and then I'll go. Now . . . in the first place you have something against Natasha; I've seen it since the day we were married. I happen to think Natasha is a good, honest person; she's straightforward and honorable. I would like you to understand that I love and respect my wife; I respect her and I demand that respect from others. She is an honest, honorable person, and whatever you imagine your grievances, I'm sorry, are just pure fabrications on your part. (*Pause.*) Secondly, you are apparently angry that I didn't finish my doctorate and that I'm not in research by now. I happen to serve on the City Council, and I think my work there is just as sacred and noble a calling as science. I'm a member of the City Council, I work hard and I have pride in my work there. (*Pause.*) Third, there's something else it's necessary for me to say . . . It is true that I mortgaged the house without your consent . . . that was wrong, I know, and I ask you to forgive me . . . That action was necessitated by my debts . . . thirty-five hundred rubles . . . I don't play cards anymore; I gave that all up long ago; my only justification is that you girls, you received an allotment and I didn't . . . I have (*Pause.*) nothing you could call income at all.

KULYGIN: (*In the door.*) Masha's not here? (*Agitatedly.*) Where is she? That's strange . . . (*Leaves.*)

Act III

ANDREI: They're not listening. Natasha is a fine, honest person. (*Walks silently up and down, then stops.*) When I was married I thought we'd be happy . . . that we'd all be happy . . . but, my God . . . (*Cries.*) Oh, my dearest, darling sisters, it's not true. Don't pay any attention to me. Don't believe me . . . (*He exits.*)

KULYGIN: (*In the door, worriedly.*) Where's Masha? Masha's not here? Astonishing. (*He exits. The tocsin sounds, the stage is empty.*)

IRINA: (*From behind the screen.*) Olya! Who's knocking on the floor?

OLGA: It's the doctor. He's drunk.

IRINA: It's been such a disturbing night! (*Pause.*) Olya! (*Looks from behind the screen.*) Did you hear? They're taking the brigade away from us. They're being transferred somewhere way away from here.

OLGA: That's only a rumor.

IRINA: We'd be left here all by ourselves . . . Olya?

OLGA: Well? .

IRINA: Darling. I respect, I do appreciate the baron. I know he's a good man. I'll marry him, I'll agree to marry him; only let's just go to Moscow! Please, please, let's go! Moscow's better than anywhere on earth! Let's go, Olya! Let's go!

CURTAIN

Act Four

The old garden of the Prozorov house. A long avenue lined on both sides with fir trees. At the end of the avenue one can see the river; on the far side of the river is a forest. On the right is the terrace of the house. On a table stand bottles and glasses. It is clear that people have been drinking a champagne toast. It is twelve noon. Occasionally people come off the road and walk toward the river through the garden. Walking briskly through the garden are five or six soldiers.

Chebutykin, in a genial mood, which does not desert him throughout the whole act, is sitting in an armchair in the garden, waiting for someone to call him. He is wearing an army cap and holding a walking stick. Irina, Kulygin, who has shaved off his moustache and is wearing a decoration on a ribbon around his neck, and Tuzenbach are standing on the terrace in order to see off Fedotik and Rodez, who are going down the steps. Both officers are in their dress uniforms.

TUZENBACH: (*Exchanging kisses with Fedotik.*) You're a good man, it's been good knowing you. (*Exchanging kisses with Rodez.*) Again, then – goodbye, my friend.

IRINA: I'll see you.

FEDOTIK: Not I'll see you, just goodbye. We won't see each other again.

KULYGIN: Who knows? (*Wipes his eyes and smiles.*) Now you've got me crying too.

IRINA: We might see each other again some day.

FEDOTIK: In ten or fifteen years, maybe? By then we'll hardly know each other, we'll just exchange an indifferent little "How do you do." (*Taking a picture.*) Stand there . . . one last time.

RODEZ: (*Embracing Tuzenbach.*) No, we're not going to see each other again . . . (*Kisses Irina's hand.*) Thank you for everything, for everything!

FEDOTIK: (*With annoyance.*) Would you just stand still!

TUZENBACH: God willing we'll get together sometime. Be sure to write us, don't forget to write.

RODEZ: (*Looking to the garden.*) Goodbye, trees! (*Shouts.*) Hup-hup!*(*Pause.*) Goodbye, echo!

KULYGIN: With any luck you'll find yourself a wife in Poland. A sweet little Polish wife to hug you up and call you her "*kokhanye.*" [Polish for sweetheart] (*Laughs.*)

FEDOTIK: (*Looking at his watch.*) We have less than an hour. Solyony's the only one going on the barge. The rest of us go with the infantry. Three batteries pull out today and three tomorrow. Then the town can have some peace and quiet.

TUZENBACH: And insufferable boredom.

RODEZ: Where's Maria Sergeevna?

KULYGIN: Masha's in the garden.

FEDOTIK: I want to say goodbye to her.

RODEZ: Goodbye, I've got to go before I start crying . . . (*Quickly embraces Tuzenbach and Kulygin, kisses Irina's hand.*) It's been wonderful.

FEDOTIK: (*To Kulygin.*) Here's something to remember us by . . . it's a notebook and pencil . . . We'll go right to the river from here . . . (*They walk away, looking back.*)

---

* "Hup-hup!" The sound used to encourage a horse to jump.

RODEZ: (*Shouting.*) Hup! Hup!

KULYGIN: (*Shouting.*) Goodbye! (*Upstage Fedotik and Rodez meet Masha and say goodbye. She leaves with them.*)

MASHA: Yes, I'll walk you.

IRINA: They're gone . . . (*Sits down on the bottom step of the terrace.*)

CHEBUTYKIN: And they forgot to say goodbye to me.

IRINA: What about you?

CHEBUTYKIN: Yes, I forgot too. But, I'll see them soon enough; I'm off tomorrow. Just one more day here. Then in a year I'll get my retirement, and come back and spend my days with you. Only one short year 'til I get my pension . . . (*Puts one newspaper in his pocket, takes out another.*) I'll come back and reform completely . . . I'll retire as a proper, country gentleman.

IRINA: I think a change is definitely in order.

CHEBUTYKIN: I'm afraid so. (*Sings quietly.*) Ta-ra-ra boom-be-ode . . . I'm sitting by the road.

KULYGIN: You're incorrigible, Ivan Romanych! Incorrigible!

CHEBUTYKIN: I know, I should have been under your tutelage; you might have made something of me.

IRINA: I can't look at Fyodor since he shaved off his moustache.

KULYGIN: Oh go on.

CHEBUTYKIN: I could tell you what your face resembles, but I don't think I will.

KULYGIN: It happens to be the fashion, *modus vivendi.* The principal shaved off his moustache, and when I became assistant principal I shaved mine off too. I don't care if anyone likes it or not. I'm content. I'm equally content with or without a moustache. (*Sits down. At the back of the stage, Andrei walks through, pushing a baby carriage with a sleeping child.*)

IRINA: I'm worried about something, Ivan Romanych. You were downtown yesterday, what happened down there?

CHEBUTYKIN: What happened? Nothing, Nonsense. (*Reads newspaper.*)

KULYGIN: They say Solyony and the baron ran into each other down by the theater yesterday.

TUZENBACH: Stop it! What's the good – really? (*Waves his hand and goes into the house.*)

KULYGIN: By the theater yesterday . . . And Solyony kept annoying the baron until finally the baron couldn't tolerate it anymore and said something Solyony took to be insulting . . .

CHEBUTYKIN: I wouldn't know. It's all nonsense, anyway.

KULYGIN: Yes, well, at a seminary once the instructor wrote on a student's paper, "Nonsense" and the student, thinking it was written in Latin, read it as "Consensus." Wonderfully amusing. (*Laughs.*) They're saying that Solyony's in love with Irina, so he despises the baron . . . Well, that's easy to understand, Irina's a lovely girl, she's a lot like Masha – they both have that pensive air. Though your disposition is gentler, Irina – which, of course, is not to say that Masha doesn't have a very good disposition herself. I do love my Masha. (*At the back of the garden, offstage:* "Halloo! Hup Hup!")

IRINA: (*Shuddering.*) I'm jumping at everything today. (*Pause.*) I'm all packed. It's ready to go off right after lunch. Then the first thing tomorrow the baron and I will be married and leave that minute for his job at the brickyard. And the day after tomorrow I'll be teaching. God willing, we can start a completely new life. I cried all during the teacher's examination from sheer joy; I just felt blessed. (*Pause.*) The cart should be here for my things by now.

KULYGIN: That's all well and good, I suppose, but somehow it isn't serious. All these theories and ideas, and nothing of real substance. But I do wish you well, with all my heart.

CHEBUTYKIN: (*Moved.*) My dear sweet, golden girl . . . you've got so far ahead of me I'll never catch up. I've just lagged behind like some migratory bird that's got too old for the trip. But you fly on, my dears, fly and God keep you. (*Pause.*) Whatever you thought you were doing, Fyodor, shaving off your moustache, it didn't work.

KULYGIN: Oh, do be quiet about it. (*Sighs.*) Well, the army's leaving today, and everything can get back to normal. Anyway, I don't care what they're saying, Masha's a good, loyal wife. I've always loved her very much; I'm thankful for whatever I have. Fate treats people so differently. There's a clerk, Kozyrev, at the office. We went to school together, but he was dropped during his junior year because the man was utterly incapable of grasping *ut consecutivum*. He's poor now, he isn't well at all; when I run into him I say, "Hello – *ut consecutivum*." And he says, "Yes, that was it, consecutivum." – and starts coughing. Whereas I've always been lucky, I'm happy, I've been awarded the Order of Stanislav, second class; and now I'm teaching the *ut consecutivum*. Obviously I'm clever, cleverer than any number of others, but it doesn't follow that that's any guarantee of happiness . . . (*Inside the house someone is playing "Maiden's Prayer."*)

IRINA: And tomorrow night I won't hear that "Maiden's Prayer" anymore. And I won't see Protopopov anymore. (*Pause.*) Protopopov's plopped himself down in the parlor again; back again today.

KULYGIN: Has our principal come yet?

IRINA: No. We sent for her. If you only knew how impossible it's been staying here by myself, without Olga . . . I know a headmistress has to live at the school, she has so many obligations, but I've been bored beyond belief. There's nothing for me to do, I've despised the room I've had . . . if I'm not going to Moscow, then that's that. That's just fate, there's nothing I can do about it . . . Everything's from God, it's true. Nikolai Lvovich had proposed to me, what was I going to do? I thought it over and came to the conclusion that really, he's a very good man – to an almost inhuman degree sometimes . . . and all of a sudden it was as if an incredible weight had been lifted off me, and I felt cheerful instead of being so uneasy all the time but better than anything I wanted to work again, just work . . . only whatever happened yesterday has thrown this mystery over everything . . .

CHEBUTYKIN: Consensus. Nonsense!

NATASHA: (*From the window.*) The principal's here.

KULYGIN: Here's the principal, let's go in. (*Goes into the house with Irina.*)

CHEBUTYKIN: (*Reads a newspaper, sings quietly.*) "Ta-ra-ra boom-be-ode . . . I'm sitting by the road." (*Masha enters. Upstage Andrei pushes the baby carriage.*)

MASHA: You're certainly taking it easy.

CHEBUTYKIN: So?

MASHA: So nothing. (*Pause.*) Did you really love Mother?

CHEBUTYKIN: Very much.

MASHA: And did she love you?

CHEBUTYKIN: (*After a pause.*) That I don't remember any more.

MASHA: Is mine here? Our cook Marfa, used to call her policeman that: Mine. Is mine here?

CHEBUTYKIN: Not yet.

MASHA: When you've taken your happiness in miserly little snippets and pieces and then you lose it all completely, as I am, it could easily make you coarse and spiteful. (*Points to her breast.*) I'm seething in here. (*Looking to Andrei who is pushing the baby carriage.*) There's our Andrei. Baby brother. Everything we'd ever prayed for is lost. A thousand people labored to hoist the bell, at what enormous expenditure of strength and money and all of a sudden the bell falls and smashes. All of a sudden for no rhyme or reason. And that's Andrei.

ANDREI: When will the house finally quiet down. What a racket.

CHEBUTYKIN: Soon. (*Looks at his watch.*) My watch is one of those old fashioned ones with a repeater. (*Winds his watch, it chimes.*) The first, second and fifth batteries will leave at exactly one o'clock . . . (*Pause.*) And I leave tomorrow.

ANDREI: For good?

CHEBUTYKIN: Who knows? Maybe I'll be back in a year. Who the hell knows? It's all the same . . . (*Far off comes the sound of a harp and a violin.*)

ANDREI: The town will be empty. We might as well stow it away under a bell-glass. (*Pause.*) What's everyone talking about? Something happened outside the theater yesterday.

CHEBUTYKIN: Nothing. Silliness. Solyony started needling the baron; the baron lost his temper and insulted him. The net result was that Solyony was obliged to challenge the baron to a duel. (*Looks at his watch.*) It's almost time . . . twelve thirty in the crown forest on the other side of the river, you can see it from here. Bang. Bang. (*Laughs.*) Solyony thinks he's Lermontov; he even writes poetry. Actually, it's no kind of joke joke, this is his third duel.

MASHA: Whose?

CHEBUTYKIN: Solyony's.

MASHA: And the baron?

CHEBUTYKIN: What about the baron?

MASHA: (*Pause.*) I can't keep anything straight, I don't think they should be allowed to go through with it. The baron could be wounded, he could be killed.

CHEBUTYKIN: The baron's a good man, but one baron more, one baron less, what's the difference? So what . . . it's all the same. (*From the other side of the garden comes a shout:* "Hallo! Hup hup!") Wait a minute. That's Skvortsov, one of the seconds. He's sitting in the boat.

ANDREI: (*Pause.*) As far as I'm concerned taking part in a duel – or attending one, even as a doctor, is immoral.

CHEBUTYKIN: It only seems like that . . . nothing in this world is real, really, we don't exist at all . . . it only seems that we exist . . . and anyway, it's all the same.

MASHA: The entire day long nothing but talk, talk, talk . . . (*Moves off.*) It isn't enough to have to live in this climate, where at any moment you'll be snowed on, one also has to endure your conversation. (*Stops.*) I can't go in there, I won't go in there . . . tell me when Vershinin gets here. (*Walks down the avenue of trees.*) The birds are leaving us already . . . (*Looks up.*) Swans or geese . . . you darling birds, my happy birds . . . (*Goes away.*)

ANDREI: Our house will be empty. The officers are leaving, you're leaving, my sister's getting married, I'll be left in the house by myself.

CHEBUTYKIN: And your wife? (*Ferapont enters with some papers.*)

ANDREI: A wife's a wife. She's honest, she's respectable, sometimes she's even thoughtful, but there's still something that drags her down to the level of some kind of low, blind, shaggy animal. She's not human, in any case. I'm talking to you as a friend; you're probably the only person I can talk to honestly, and I do love Natasha, of course, but there're still times when she seems so astonishingly vulgar, that I simply have no hope, I have no idea what I feel, or how I could possibly love her, or at least used to love . . .

CHEBUTYKIN: (*Standing up.*) Well, brother, I'm going to be leaving tomorrow. We may never see each other again, so take my advice. Put on your hat, take up your walking stick and walk. Walk right on by, don't even look back. And the further the better. (*Solyony crosses the back of the stage with two officers. Seeing Chebutykin, he turns toward him. The officers keep walking.*)

SOLYONY: Doctor, it's time. It's twelve thirty already. (*Shakes hands with Andrei.*)

CHEBUTYKIN: Yes, and I'm sick of all of you. (*To Andrei.*) If anyone asks for me, Andryusha, I'll be right back . . . (*Sighs.*) Well, well, well!

SOLYONY: "Before he even made a peep, / The bear was on him in a leap." (*Moves off with him.*) What are you groaning about, old man?

CHEBUTYKIN: Never mind.

SOLYONY: How do you feel?

CHEBUTYKIN: (*Angrily.*) Fresh as butter.

SOLYONY: Don't get worked up over nothing, old man. I'll only indulge myself a little; I'll wing him like a woodchuck. (*Takes out the cologne and sprinkles his hands.*) I've used a whole bottle today and my hands still stink. My hands stink like something dead. (*Pause.*) Ah, well. Remember the poem? "And he, the rebel, seeks the storm as if in storms resided peace."*

*Lermentov: the closing two lines of his twelve-line poem, *The Sail.*

CHEBUTYKIN: Yes. "Before he even made a peep, / The bear was on him with a leap." (*Goes out with Solyony. Shouts are heard;* "Hup hup!" *Enter Andrei and Ferapont.*)

FERAPONT: Some papers to sign.

ANDREI: (*Nervously.*) Leave me alone. Leave me alone. Please. (*Exits.*)

FERAPONT: That's why we have papers, so men can have something to sign. (*Goes off U. Enter Irina and Tuzenbach, who is wearing a straw hat. Kulygin crosses the stage shouting,* "Yoo-hoo, Masha, Yoo-hoo.")

TUZENBACH: I imagine that's the only man in town who's glad the army's leaving.

IRINA: Understandably. (*Pause.*) Our town's going to be deserted.

TUZENBACH: (*Looking at his watch.*) My dear, I have to go now.

IRINA: Where to?

TUZENBACH: I have to go downtown, then . . . see some friends off.

IRINA: No you don't . . . Nikolai , why are you so distracted? What happened outside the theater yesterday?

TUZENBACH: I'll be back in an hour and I'll be with you again. (*Kisses her hand.*) My dear . . . (*Looks into her face.*) I've loved you for five years now and I still can't get used to it; you always seem more marvelous to me; what lovely hair! What eyes! I'll take you off tomorrow and we'll work, we'll have a fine life; we'll have the life I've dreamed of. You'll be happy. There's only one thing, only one thing – you don't love me.

IRINA: That isn't in my power. I'll be your wife, I"ll be faithful and obedient, but not in love, what can I do? (*Cries.*) I've never been in love in my life. Oh, I've dreamed about love, I've dreamed for years, day and night, but my heart is like some rich man's piano that's been kept locked so long the key's been lost. (*Pause.*) You seem so restless.

TUZENBACH: I couldn't get to sleep all night. There's never been anything in my life so terrible it really frightened me, but I'm tormented by that lost key; it won't let me sleep . . . Say something to me. (*Pause.*) Say something to me.

IRINA: What? Say what? What?

TUZENBACH: Something.

IRINA: Enough! Enough!

TUZENBACH: Such silly, such silly little things sometimes in life seem so important for no reason. You laugh them off the same way you always have, and tell yourself they're silly, but you still don't seem to have the strength to stop thinking about them. Oh, let's not talk about it. Just enjoy being here. I feel like it's the first time in my life I've really seen those fir trees and those maples and birches; and they're looking back at me with such curiosity, waiting. What beautiful trees. They deserve only beautiful lives to be lived around them. (*A shout:* "Hey. Hup-hup!") I've got to go, it's time . . . look at that tree, it's dead, but it still stands there rocking in the wind with the others. I think it would be like that with me. If I die I'll still be a part of those lives around me in some way. Goodbye, darling . . . (*Kisses her hands.*) Those papers you gave me are on my desk, under the calendar.

IRINA: I'll come with you.

TUZENBACH: (*Agitatedly.*) No, no. (*Quickly moves off, stops in the tree-lined avenue.*) Irina!

IRINA: What!

TUZENBACH: (*Not knowing what to say.*) I didn't have coffee this morning.

Could you please ask them to make me some? (*Goes out quickly. Irina stands lost in thought, then walks U. and sits in a swing. Enter Andrei with the baby carriage. Ferapont appears.*)

ANDREI: Oh, where is it? What's happened to that time when I was young and positive, alive; when I dreamed, I had ideas, when the world around me and the future was bright with hope? Why do we become so dull and boring, almost before we've started to live. Lazy, indifferent, useless, morose . . . Our town has stood for two hundred years, a hundred thousand people live here, and there's not one who isn't exactly like the other; not one zealot, past or present, not one scholar, not an artist, not one even vaguely distinctive person who might arouse envy or a burning desire to follow him, to model your life on his . . . All they do is eat, drink, sleep and die . . . them some others are born and they eat, drink, sleep and in order not to go totally numb with boredom they brighten their lives with gossip, vodka, gambling and intrigue. The wives cheat on their husbands and the husbands lie and pretend they don't see it, pretend they don't hear it, and this mindboggling vulgarity inevitably crushes the children, completely quenching any spark they might have in them until the children become the same interchangeable zombies as their mothers and fathers. (*Angry, to Ferapont.*) What do you want?

FERAPONT: Say what? Papers to sign.

ANDREI: I'm sick of you.

FERAPONT: (*Handing the papers.*) The porter over at the Council said they had two hundred degrees of frost in Petersburg last winter.

ANDREI: The life we live is disgusting, but at least when I think about the future there's hope. There at last is some light, space, and way off in the distance the sun comes up, and I can see freedom; I see my children and me becoming free from this sloth, from this kvass, from this goose and cabbage, from these after-dinner naps and this parasitic life . . .

FERAPONT: Said two thousand people froze to death . . . Everybody was scared witless. Petersburg or Moscow. Don't remember.

ANDREI: (*Seized by compassion.*) My dear sisters, my wonderful sisters! (*Through tears.*) Masha, my sister . . .

NATASHA: (*At the window.*) Who's that making so much noise? Is that you, Andryusha? You'll wake up little Sophie. *Il ne faut pas faire du bruit, las Sophie est dormee deja. Vous etes un ours.* [Don't make noise. Sophie sleeps already. You are a bear.] (*Getting angry.*) If you want to talk, give the carriage to someone else. Ferapont, take the carriage from master.

FERAPONT: Yes, Ma'am. (*Takes the buggy.*)

ANDREI: (*Flustered.*) I was talking quietly.

NATASHA: (*Behind the window, talking tenderly to the little boy.*) Bobik! Bobik, you rascal! Naughty Bobik!

ANDREI: (*Glancing over the papers.*) All right, I'll look them over and sign whatever has to be signed, then you can take them back to the office. (*Goes into the house reading the papers. Ferapont wheels the buggy to the garden.*)

NATASHA: (*Behind the window.*) Bobik, can you say "Mommy?" You sweetheart. And look who this is! Who is this? Is this Aunt Olya? Say, "Hello, Aunt Olya!" (*Wandering musicians, a man and a girl, are playing a violin and a harp. Vershinin, Olga and Anfisa enter from the house. They listen silently for a minute, Irina joins them.*)

OLGA: Our garden's like a thoroughfare. Everyone walks through or rides through. Nanny, give the musicians something.

ANFISA: (*Gives something to the musicians. The musicians bow and go out.*) Poor people, I know. You wouldn't bother making music if you had enough to eat. (*To Irina.*) Hello, Arisha! (*Kisses her.*) Oh, my little darling, what a life I'm having! What a wonderful life! There I am at the school with Olya, in that wonderful free apartment. God's provided for my old age. I've never lived so good in my life, sinner that I am. A big rent-free apartment, I have my own room, my own bed. I wake up in the middle of the night and then realize, Oh, Lord, Holy Mother of God, I'm the luckiest woman on earth!

VERSHININ: We're leaving now, Olga Sergeevna. It's time for me to go. (*Pause.*) I wish you all the all the . . . where's Masha?

IRINA: Somewhere in the garden. I'll go look.

VERSHININ: Please. I have to be on time.

ANFISA: I'll go look for her. Mashenka, yoo-hoo! (*Goes out with Irina to the back of the garden.*)

VERSHININ: Everything comes to an end. Now we have to say our goodbyes. (*Looks at his watch.*) The town gave us a luncheon; we drank champagne, the mayor made a speech, I ate and listened, but my heart was here with you . . . (*Looks around the garden.*) I've got so used to being with you.

OLGA: Will we see you again sometime?

VERSHININ: Probably not. (*Pause.*) My wife and two little girls will stay here another month or two . . . please if something happens or if they need anything . . .

OLGA: Yes, yes, of course, don't think about it. (*Pause.*) There won't be a soldier left in town tomorrow; it'll all just be a memory, and, of course, it will be up to us to begin our lives all over again . . . (*Pause.*) Everything has a way of turning out wrong, doesn't it? I didn't want to be made principal, and I was . . . so now going to Moscow is impossible for me.

VERSHININ: So . . . thank you for everything. Forgive me if everything wasn't what – I've talked too much, I know, forgive that, too; try not to hold it against me.

OLGA: (*Wiping her eyes.*) Why on earth doesn't Masha come?

VERSHININ: What more could there possibly be for me to say in parting? What else is there left for me to talk about? (*Laughs.*) Life is difficult. It may seem bleak and hopeless to many of us, but still we have to admit that it's becoming steadily clearer and lighter; obviously the time isn't far off when there will be light everywhere. (*Looks at his watch.*) Time for me to go, it's time! Man has been so preoccupied with wars, filling his life with campaigns and invasions and victories, and now that he doesn't have that diversion it's left an enormous emptiness in his life. Just now we have nothing to fill that emptiness with, but he is searching, passionately, and of course, someday he'll find it. Oh, let it be soon. (*Pause.*) If, you know, we could educate the diligent and give some sense of diligence to the educated. However, it's time for me . . .

OLGA: She's coming. (*Masha enters.*)

VERSHININ: I've come to say goodbye . . . (*Olga goes to the side, out of the way.*)

MASHA: (*Looking him in the face.*) Goodbye. (*A prolonged kiss.*)

OLGA: Come on, come on. (*Masha sobs violently.*)

VERSHININ: Write me . . . Don't forget! Let me go! . . . it's time . . . Olga Sergeevna, take her; it's already . . . time . . . I'm late. (*Deeply moved, he kisses Olga's hands, embraces Masha once more and quickly leaves.*)

OLGA: Come on, Masha, stop. Darling, please. (*Enter Kulygin.*)

KULYGIN: (*In confusion.*) It's all right. Let her cry, let . . . My Masha's good, my Masha's dear . . . you're my wife and I'm happy, whatever happens . . . I'm not complaining, I'm not doing anything to hurt you. Olga's my witness . . . we'll pick up our lives just as we were and I'll never say a word, not a sign . . .

MASHA: "An oak tree grows" (*Trying to restrain the sobs.*) "in a sheltered cove, a golden chain wound around it . . . A golden chain would around it" . . . . I'm losing my mind . . . "an oak tree . . . in a sheltered cove."

OLGA: Just calm down, Masha, calm down. Give her some water.

MASHA: I'm not crying anymore.

KULYGIN: She's not crying now . . . she's fine . . .

MASHA: "an oak tree grows in a sheltered cove, a golden chain wound around it, a golden cat . . ." I'm mixing everything up . . . (*Drinks water.*) What a God awful life . . . I don't need anything, I'll be all right now . . . it's all the same . . . what does that mean, "in a sheltered cove?" . . . why do those words keep coming into my head? My thoughts are all mixed up. (*Enter Irina.*)

OLGA: Calm down, Masha. There, that's sensible . . . let's go inside . . .

MASHA: (*Angry.*) I'm not going in there. (*Sobs, immediately stops.*) I am never going in that house again. Never.

IRINA: We can sit here together, we don't have to talk. I'm leaving tomorrow.

KULYGIN: (*Pause.*) Yesterday I confiscated a false beard from one of the third-grade boys . . . (*Puts them on.*) I look like the German teacher . . . (*Laughs.*) don't you think? The boys are funny.

MASHA: Actually you do look like the German.

OLGA: (*Laughing.*) Yes. (*Masha cries.*)

IRINA: Don't, Masha.

KULYGIN: Very much . . . (*Enter Natasha.*)

NATASHA: (*To the maid.*) What? Protopopov is going to sit with little Sophie, let Andrei take Bobik for a walk. There's so much bother with those children. (*To Irina.*) Irina, you're going to leave tomorrow. I'm sorry. You should at least stay another week. (*Seeing Kulygin with the beard, she shrieks. He laughs and takes off the beard.*) Oh, you! You scared me! (*To Irina.*) I've got so used to you, don't think for a minute it's going to be easy to let you leave us. I'm going to have Andrei and his violin moved into your room. He can play it in there. And we'll put little Sophie in his room. She's such a wonderful, sweet child! What a little girl! She looked up at me with those eyesies and said, "Mama!"

KULYGIN: She is, she's a marvelous child.

NATASHA: So tomorrow I'll be all alone here. (*Sighs.*) The first thing I do, I want to have that row of fir trees taken out, and then that maple . . . it's so forbidding in the evening. (*To Irina.*) Darling, that belt doesn't suit you at all . . . It's so bland . . . you should have something to brighten you up. And I'm going to have flowers, flowers everywhere, with a wonderful fragrance. (*Going to the house. To the maid, sternly.*) May I ask what a fork is doing out here? (*Shouts.*) I don't want to hear it!

KULYGIN: There she goes. (*Offstage a band is playing a march. Everyone listens.*)

OLGA: They're leaving. (*Chebutykin enters.*)

MASHA: Our men are leaving. Well . . . so be it. Happy journey to them! (*To her husband.*) We have to go home. Where's my hat and cape?

KULYGIN: I took them in . . . I'll get them. (*Goes into the house.*)

Act IV

OLGA: Yes, we can all go to our homes. It's time.

CHEBUTYKIN: Olga Sergeevna!

OLGA: What? (*Pause.*) What?

CHEBUTYKIN: Nothing . . . I don't know how to tell you . . . (*Whispers in her ear.*)

OLGA: (*Aghast.*) It's impossible!

CHEBUTYKIN: Yes . . . That's what happened. I'm worn out, it's done me in, no more; I don't want to talk . . . (*With irritation.*) Anyway, it's all the same.

MASHA: What happened?

OLGA: (*Puts her arms around Irina.*) What a horrible day, darling, I don't know how to tell you.

IRINA: What? Just say it. What? For God's sake. (*Cries.*)

CHEBUTYKIN: The baron has just been killed in a duel.

IRINA: (*Crying quietly.*) I knew, I knew . . .

CHEBUTYKIN: (*Sitting down on a bench at the back of the stage.*) I'm exhausted . . (*Takes a newspaper from his pocket.*) Let her cry . . . (*Sings quietly.*) "Ta-ra-ra-boom-be-ode. I'm sitting by the road" . . . It's all just the same. (*The three sisters stand huddled close to each other.*)

MASHA: The band is playing. They're leaving us. One of them has gone from us completely, completely, forever . . . And we're left alone to pick up our lives again. I'll go on living, sisters . . . You have to live . . . The birds are migrating. Just the way they have every spring and fall for a thousand years. They have no idea why, they just fly and they'll go on flying forever, for thousands of years more until God finally reveals his mystery to them.

IRINA: (*Laying her head on Olga's breast.*) Someday people will know why life's the way it is, why it's all so painful. Nothing will be a mystery anymore. But 'til that time comes we still have to live . . . We've got to work, just work. I'm going to go on by myself tomorrow to teach at the school, and give my life to those who might need it. It's autumn now, before you know it, it'll be winter, everything will be covered with snow, but I'll be working, I'll be working . . .

OLGA: (*Holding both sisters.*) The band is playing so brightly, so cheerfully, that you want to live. Oh, my God! Time will pass, we'll be gone forever, they'll forget us, forget our faces, our voices, forget how many of us there were. But what we've suffered will be transformed into such gladness by the people who live after us . . . There'll be peace on earth, and happiness, and they'll think about us kindly and be grateful for us. Oh, dear sisters, our lives aren't nearly finished. We'll live! The band is playing so brightly, so happily and it seems just a little longer and we'll find out why we live, why life is so painful. If we could know that, if we could know!

CHEBUTYKIN: (*Sings quietly.*) "Ta-ra-ra-boom-be-ode, I'm sitting by the road" . . . (*Reading the newspaper.*) It's all the same! It's all the same!

OLGA: If we could only know, if we could only know!

CURTAIN